I0189645

IMAGES
of America

FOSTORIA

OHIO

Volume II

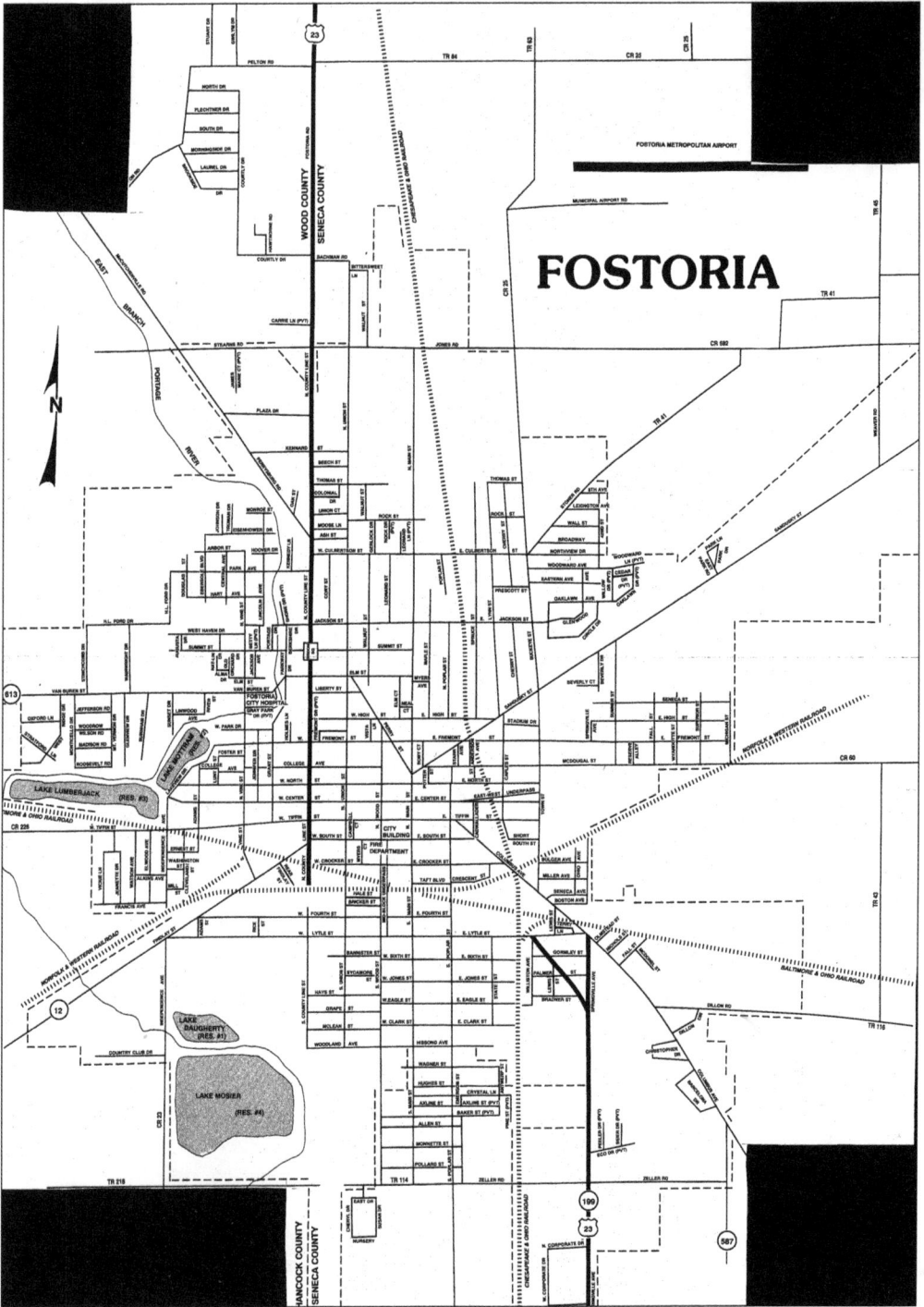

A recent map of Fostoria, Ohio.

IMAGES
of America

FOSTORIA

OHIO

Volume II

as told by Paul H. Krupp

COMMEMORATING
The State of Ohio's Bicentennial (1803–2003)
and
The City of Fostoria's Sesquicentennial (1854–2004)

ARCADIA
PUBLISHING

Copyright © 2002 by Nathan G. Krupp.
ISBN 978-1-5316-1359-4

Published by Arcadia Publishing
Charleston, South Carolina

Library of Congress Catalog Card Number: Applied For.

For all general information contact Arcadia Publishing at:
Telephone 843-853-2070
Fax 843-853-0044
E-mail sales@arcadiapublishing.com
For customer service and orders:
Toll-Free 1-888-313-2665

Visit us on the Internet at www.arcadiapublishing.com

Cover description: Looking north on Main Street from the corner of Tiffin and Main around 1900.

THIS 2-VOLUME SERIES OF WRITINGS ON FOSTORIA, OHIO, BY PAUL H. KRUPP, WOULD NOT BE A REALITY WITHOUT THE EFFORTS OF MANY, BUT ESPECIALLY RAY DELL, NORMAN GIBAT, GEORGE GRAY, AND DAVID KRUPP. THIS SECOND VOLUME IS GRATEFULLY DEDICATED TO THEM.

Norman Gibat, George Gray, Ray Dell, and David Krupp.

CONTENTS

ACKNOWLEDGMENTS

From 1977 through 1989, Paul H. Krupp wrote a weekly column in the *Fostoria Review Times* about the history of Fostoria, Ohio. Entitled "Potluck," it was about the people, places, and events that are the history of this town in northwestern Ohio.

When his son Nathan began to sense that something needed to be done to put these articles into book form, he first contacted Clarence Pennington and George Gray. They gave much helpful counsel and encouragement.

In 1996, a committee was formed to begin working on this project. This committee included George Gray, owner of Gray Printing Company, and president of the Fostoria Area Historical Society; Clarence Pennington, publisher of the local newspaper, the *Fostoria Review Times*, which first published Paul's articles; Norman Gibat, owner of Noguska computer company, and former neighbor of the Krupps; Nathan and David Krupp, Paul's two sons; Janet Therriault, his only daughter; and Nancy Adams Slaymaker, a cousin and community leader.

Much thanks goes to Norman Gibat for coordinating a host of volunteers, including Susan Thompson, Marilyn Beers, and Carol Wangler, who typed all of the original articles on computer, the first step in moving toward publication. Ben Pohman got it all ready for a web site, which you can access at Fostoria.org.

Paul's son, Nathan, did the editing of the articles. He attempted to select the articles of greatest interest to the most readers and to delete duplicate or less-important material. This was no easy task, and we hope you are happy with the final selection of material and photos. The date on which the article originally appeared is included with the article title. If there is more than one date, it means that the article is a combination of several original articles. In some cases an original photo could not be found and we had to make an appropriate substitution. Nate's wife, Joanne, spent many hours giving editorial assistance and proofreading.

Locating the original photos was a task performed by David Krupp, Ray Dell, George Gray, and Leonard Skonecki. A number of present and former Fostoria residents were very helpful to search and find needed photos, including Doris Norris and Penny Justice of the Fostoria McClean Public Library and Hazel Coppler-Rowles, Tim Ash, and Candyland.

We are most grateful to those in Fostoria who promoted and sold the first volume: Readmore Bookstore, the Historical Museum, the Glass Museum, the Arts Council, Pharm Pharmacy, and R&L Stained Glass; with additional promotion done by Mike McKitrick of WFOB and Linda Woodland of the *Review Times*.

We are grateful to Mayor John Davoli for making this second volume part of the Fostoria Sesquicentennial celebration of 2004.

It has been a delight to work with Arcadia Publishing.

Pictured here are Nathan Krupp and his wife, Joanne.

INTRODUCTION

Paul Howard Krupp was born in Fostoria, Ohio, on May 8, 1905. He lived his entire life in this small industrial town in northwestern Ohio. His father died of tuberculosis when he was only three. They were not a wealthy family. His mother went to work in the garment factory to support Paul and his two sisters, Ruth and Virginia. One of his first recollections was pulling his little wagon along the railroad track and picking up pieces of coal to heat their small home.

While still in high school Paul went to work for the local newspaper, the *Fostoria Review*. On July 31, 1931, he married Cleo May Allis of Tiffin, Ohio. He held various positions with the paper until 1941, when he went to work in the sales department of the Fostoria Pressed Steel. He retired from there in 1970.

After retirement he began a series of articles in the *Fostoria Review Times* on the history of Fostoria. This column, entitled "Potluck," ran from 1977 through 1989. It was "the talk of the town." As he said in his January 12, 1977, introductory article:

As I start thinking about my 'new assignment,' it is almost like starting another chapter in my life, and it makes me turn in retrospect to my early association with this newspaper when it was the *Fostoria Daily Review*. Fred M. Hopkins was editor and publisher; Clayton Kinsey, advertising manager; Arthur Murray and Ella McNailey (Aldrich) were news editors. That was the lineup when I started as a carrier boy back in 1917 or 1918.

When I graduated from Fostoria High in 1923, I went to work for the *Review* full-time, 'printers devil' at first. I had been given a scholarship to Wooster College, through the efforts of my pastor, T. Howard McDowell of the Presbyterian Church, but had to forego college to support my family. My mother had had a stroke and a younger sister was still in school. So, I learned the printing trade, learned to run the job presses, the big press, and to make-up the paper. Later I assisted in the editorial and advertising department. In 1941 I left the *Review Times* to work for the Fostoria Pressed Steel. So, now after 35 years, here I am back at my first love. They say if printers ink gets in your blood, you are hooked!

Paul went to be with his Lord on January 26, 1999, at the age of 93. His articles have been edited to remove duplicate information and are now offered in this 2-volume book form.

The editing, combining, and arranging of the articles for these books was done by Paul's oldest son, Nathan. Nate graduated from Fostoria High School in 1953. In 1957, he received a Bachelor of Science degree in Mechanical Engineering from Purdue University, where he was Student Body President his senior year. After two years as an officer in the Navy's Civil Engineer Corps, he and his wife, Joanne, have spent over 40 years in missionary work that has taken them from the ghettos of Chicago to many nations on every continent. They live in Salem, Oregon, and currently oversee a Christian publishing enterprise, Preparing the Way Publishers.

Once in Dad Krupp's later years he said to Nate, "Fostoria has been good to you. You have a debt to pay to this town." Some years later those words came back to Nate, as he began working with a local committee to produce these two volumes. He has spent several years working on this 2-volume series project. This effort is the payment of "his debt" to Fostoria. The whole process has been a delight, especially working with the local Fostorians, all of whom have been so helpful.

"Thank you to all of my dear friends in Fostoria, Ohio."

This is not a complete history of Fostoria. We could only work with the articles that Dad wrote. We pray that these two volumes will be a blessing to all Fostorians everywhere.

Paul Knopp

One

OUR HISTORIC STREETS

PLANK ROADS
(November 15, 1984)

Sandusky, referred to originally as Lower Sandusky, was well situated as a central trading point for collecting produce and selling merchandise for an area extending southward more than halfway to Tiffin, eastward to at least halfway to Bellevue, north almost to Port Clinton, and west halfway or more to Perrysburg, and southwest as far as Risdon and Rome (now Fostoria). Products were brought to Sandusky for sale or exchange and for shipment by way of the Sandusky River; then on Lake Erie to Buffalo, and finally to New York City.

Unfortunately, the dirt roads, excepting the Maumee and the Western Reserve turnpike, were never good, and much of the year they were impassable. Consequently the time and expense of hauling heavy loads of wheat, corn, and pork was considerable and reduced the value of the products. The idea of building plank roads was born. The Lower Sandusky Plank Road Company chartered with capital stock of $100,000 in shares of $50 each. The plan of the Lower Sandusky Plank Road Company was to build a road from the south termination of Front Street in Sandusky, southward along the Sandusky River to the south line of Edward Tindall's land; thence southwesterly to Bettsville, and then to Rome (now Fostoria), with a branch starting from the south line of Tindall's land south to Tiffin. Sawmills in the vicinity were engaged for exclusive production of planks and strings for the road.

The form of the plank road, when finished, was that of a turnpike, well-graded and ditched. The crown or flat surface of the top of the pike was 18 feet wide. The planks were 8 feet long and 2 inches thick of the best white or bur oak, laid crosswise on firm stringers embedded in the earth. On one side of the crown a good earth road was left for use in dry weather and for the use by teams in all weather if they had to turn out for another team to pass, which was entitled to the plank track.

Even though the era of the Plank Road brought renewed vigor to the entire area for which it was constructed, its destiny was doomed by the development of a system of railroads through northwestern Ohio and was abandoned early in 1860.

This photo shows a typical Plank Road in use, with an unimproved road beside the improved portion to accommodate vehicles that had to turn off the main road, allowing the most privileged team to continue.

MUD STREETS BECOME BRICK
(September 21, 1978)

Fostoria's original streets were dirt—mud when it rained! The first drainage for our town was by open ditches, and the first one was from the southeast corner of Fremont and Perry streets, thence west along Fremont Street to Portage Creek. That first segment was completed in October of 1856—and the cost was the amazing amount of $68.36. The first improvement to Main Street was authorized by city council in 1859. Fifty carloads of stone were used on Main Street between Perry and Tiffin Streets, at a cost of $4 per load.

In 1870, city council created a board of improvement and employed a city engineer, James Lewis, appointed by Mayor Bricker. Soon after that the first underground sewer was authorized. It was a main sewer that began at Potter and Sandusky Streets, thence across Perry Street and on west to College Avenue, then north on Countyline to Fremont and west to Portage Creek.

During the 1880s, there were not any hardtop streets yet. After a hard rain it was almost impossible for a horse-drawn vehicle to traverse them. During the dry season it was conversely nearly as bad because of the dust created by the horse-drawn vehicles. On Main Street, prior to paving, the dust was laid by a large tank-type sprinkling wagon, which applied water daily for a cost of $1 per month for each business establishment. Gradually, sewers were extended and Fostoria's streets were improved by one or more methods—some being cement, others macadam, and a few wood blocks saturated with preservative, but mostly were brick. Today, Fostoria has 85 miles of hardtop streets. Those that were paved with bricks formed the substantial base for the successive layers of asphalt that have been applied in later years.

A great contribution to the improvement of Fostoria's streets was made years ago by Charles "Gene" Wilson, who earned the title of Champion Street Brick Layer for this area—perhaps nationwide. Gene was credited with laying an average of 225 tons of paving bricks per day. Each one measured 3 1/2 x 4 x 8 1/2 inches and weighed 10 pounds, much heavier than normal construction bricks. It took a crew of men just to keep Wilson supplied with the bricks as he worked with both hands picking them up and laying them in a checkerboard pattern. As a boy, I remember seeing him work—no lost motions—and oh how they went down. And oh how the perspiration poured off him. Wilson once set a record of laying 132 of the bricks in 55 seconds, which bettered his average record of 225 tons per day by a large margin. He was written up in "Ripley's Believe it or Not." He laid the bricks on Sandusky Street from Main, east to the railroad tracks in one afternoon. That's a lot of 10-pound bricks to handle!

Here is a view of Main Street at Center looking south, c.1845. The building at the far right was the first brick structure in Fostoria. On the left side of the photo (foreground) was the site of the Hays building, later to be rebuilt as the Hays Hotel. The large 2-story structure at center left is the corner of Main and Tiffin Streets, where the Commercial Bank is now. Note the mud streets. Pictured in the corner is Charles "Gene" Wilson.

COUNTYLINE STREET
(October 9, 1980, February 9, 1984, and March 26, 1987)

Countyline Street was originally the Main Street for Risdon, one of the villages that merged to become Fostoria. In the fall of 1832, John Gorsuch plotted the village of Risdon, surveyed for him by David Risdon. It was located on the northwest corner of Section 6, Township 2 north, Range 13 east. Originally the 40 acres deeded to John Gorsuch on March 31, 1831, by the State of Ohio, was part of a plan to extend the Miami Canal from Dayton to Lake Erie. In its early history Risdon touted a hotel, stagecoach stop, brickyard, school, church, cemetery, grocery, doctor, and houses.

David Risdon was born at Rupert, Vermont, on July 6, 1788, son of Josiah Risdon and his wife, Martha Cochran Risdon. David had worked as a surveyor with his brother, Orange, and father prior to the War of 1812. After the close of the war in 1814, he worked as a surveyor in western New York for a few years, and then came to Seneca County, Ohio, in April of 1820 to survey land for the United States government.

Rome, another little village, was plotted on the east half of the southwest quarter of the same section as Risdon by David Risdon for Roswell Crocker in August 1832. Years later the arm of the big swamp separating the two villages was filled and the two became one in 1854. Since the people in both Risdon and Rome would not accept the name of the other village, they compromised by naming the town Fostoria after Charles W. Foster, a leading citizen and the first mayor.

This photo shows the plaque at the corner of Countyline and Summit Streets, an area of the village of Risdon, which was set aside as a public square, never to be used for any other purpose—and so it remains today.

TOWN OF RISDON

JACKSON STREET

WOOD CO.

Wood County _ _ _ _ _ _ _
Hancock County

Hancock Co.

Seneca Co.

| 60. | 51. | 50. | 31. | | 30. | | 11. | 10. | 1. |

32. 29.

33. 28.

34. 27.

59. 52. 49. 35. 26. 12. 9. 2.

36. **Risdon** 25.

MAIN CROSS
(Now Summit St.) **Square** **MAIN CROSS**
(Now Summit St.)

37. 24.

58. 53. 48. 38. 23. 13. 8. 3.

39. 22.

40. 21.

57. 54. 47. 41. 20. 14. 7. 4.

42. 19.

CREEK

PORTAGE

ELM STREET **ELM STREET**

43. 18.

56. 55. 46 44. 17. 15. 6. 5

45. 16.

MAIN STREET (Now Countyline Street)

Hancock Co.
Seneca Co. (Now Countyline Street)

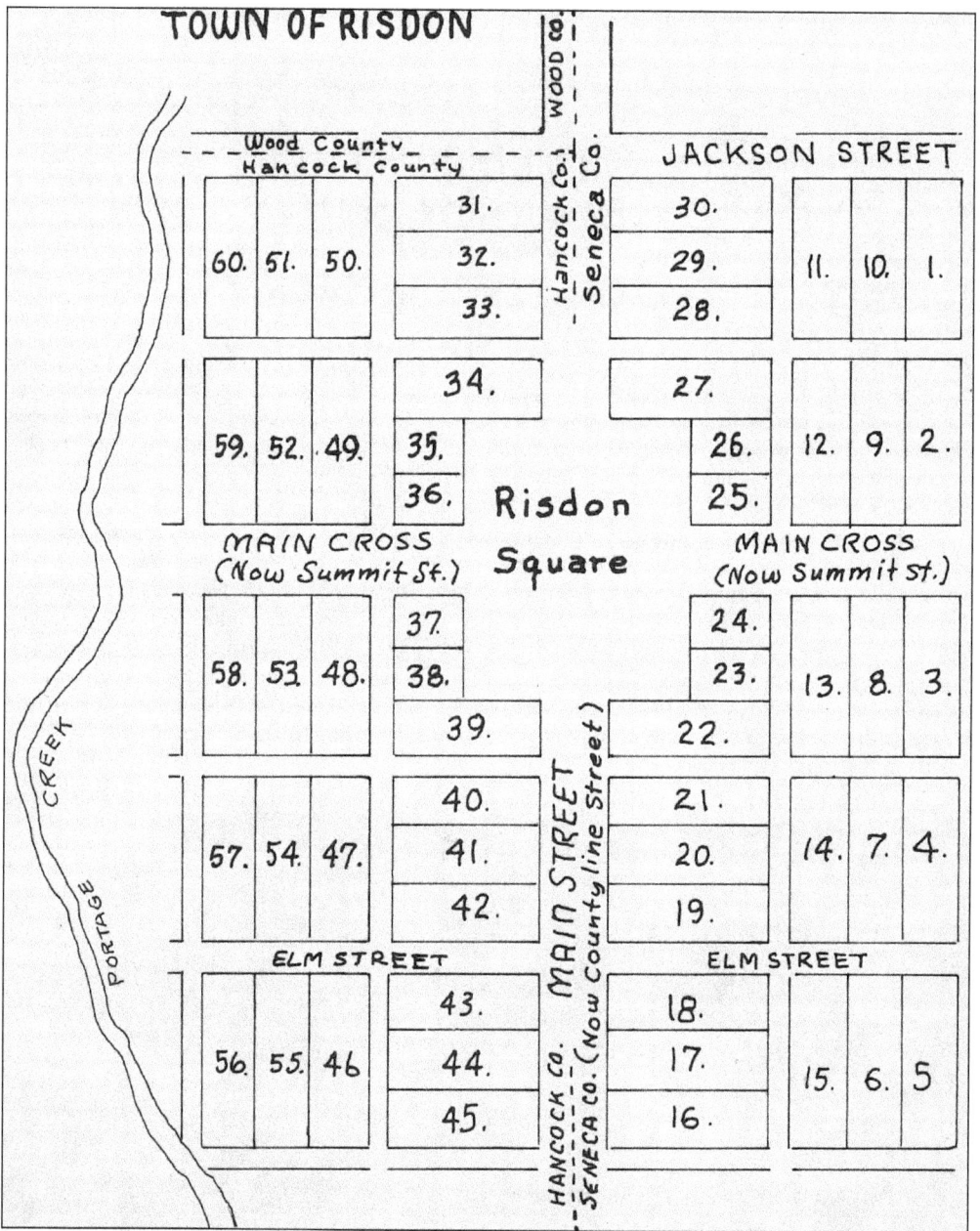

This map shows the 40 acres of land that were originally the village of Risdon. Today's Countyline Street was Risdon's Main Street.

14

PERRY STREET
(September 28, October 5, 12, 1978, and February 22, 1979)

Let's start our look at Perry Street by looking at the corner of Main, Perry, and Sandusky Streets—once called Times Square, because the *Fostoria Times*, one of two newspapers in Fostoria years ago, occupied the building that was located where Standard Oil filling station is now. Prior to occupancy by the *Times*, the building housed the W.D. Robbins Marble Shop, which made grave markers, marble table tops for antique furniture, so much sought after today, and perhaps marble windowsills. When the *Times* was purchased by the *Review*, it was the start of the transformation of Times Square corner. The Times Building, owned by Roscoe Carle, publisher, was sold and eventually demolished to become a site for successive filling stations. Notice the horse and buggy, the streetcar tracks (Toledo, Fostoria, and Findlay), and the street paved with bricks.

Let's cross to the other side of Perry Street. A photo shows the Poley Stucco Flats. About 1910, it was the home of the Union Delivery service (see page 46 for more on this). After the delivery service went out of existence, enterprising Joe Poley turned that part of his building into a professional wrestling arena. Your editor, as will many readers, remembers the headliners—the Black Panther, Martino Angelo, Masked Marvel and many others. Joseph Poley was the head of Joseph Poley and Company: Marble and Granite Works. The company also made street curbing, large quantities of which were used for Fostoria's streets.

Moving further north on Perry Street we have a house where the H.L. Porter family lived—yes, the same Porter family that started the Dye Works and Dry Cleaning business in 1889, in the frame building to the left of their residence. Porter's business stayed in the family and in the same place for 74 years, until it was purchased by Charles Lyburtus, a long-time employee at Porters. The 2-story frame building to the left of Porter's housed a barber shop, where haircuts cost 15¢ and shaves 10¢. The small 1-story structure to the left was a shoe repair shop, probably run by Earl French. The 2-story structure with the outside entrance for upstairs housed a second-hand store on the first floor, probably run by Josep Henning. The Dehaber building stands there now.

Another photo is the Perry Street House—a hotel that was a landmark for many years, during a time when Fostoria had six to eight hotels. The house was occupied by a couple generations of the George W. Might family, then later purchased and occupied by the Pete Tsantle family, who also acquired the hotel property.

The final photo is a nostalgic view of the old Central High School at the corner of Perry and High Streets.

Many changes have taken place at both corners of Perry and Elm streets. Where Mr. B's is now there was once a filling station, operated for many years by Mr. Blose. On the opposite corner, there have been many grocery businesses in the two separate buildings that still stand there, including Risdon Meat Market, A&P, McArthur, Larry Firestine, and Kenneth Thrailkill.

Here is a view of the old Times Building with Main Street looking north on the right and Perry Street looking north on the left.

This photo shows the Poley Stucco Flats. After Poley had gone out of the monument business, many others took over space in his building, including the following: Murphy and Hummer Shoe Repair, Dozer Concrete Vault Works, G.L. Kline Co. Chair Rental, J.M. Schlenker Barber Shop, F.A. Watts-Naturopathy, Duffield's Music Center, Sara Jane's Dance School, L and S Hobby and Yarn Shop, Edwards Dry Cleaning, Homerick Studio, Davis Bicycle Shop, The Fostoria Auto Club, Fostoria Electric, Head Shed Barber Shop, and Robert M. Green Insurance. The building had a wooden veranda for the upstairs residential apartments.

Seen here is Perry Street House, a hotel. When the old hotel and house were demolished, Jim Tsantles, son of Pete, operated a used car lot on the site for a while and eventually the Commercial Bank purchased all of the land where the new bank was built.

Here is a nostalgic view of Central High School area at Perry and High.

Main Street

(Much of this material is from Paul Krupp's article, "Stroll Down Main Street of Yesteryear," which appeared on December 26, 1985, in a special *Review Times*' 125th Anniversary Edition; but is supplemented by material from articles on September 6, 1979; February 5, April 30, May 7, June 25, and September 3, 10, 17, 1981.)

This photo was taken on November 11, 1918, at the end of World War I, at the junction of Main, Sandusky, and Perry Streets, looking south down Main Street. Between Sandusky and North there once stood a row of 2-story frame buildings, where a variety of business establishments were located on the first floors and residential quarters on the second.

Seen here is the northwest corner of Main and North, *c.* 1890. The *Daily Democrat* newspaper office was upstairs. Eventually, it became the *Fostoria Daily Times*. The corner store was J.L. Faulhaber Hardware, and next-door was the Kentucky Liquor Store.

The Every Man's Bible Class, founded by Reverend E.L. Miley, met every Sunday morning in the Colonial Theatre. It drew large crowds, including many who had no church affiliation. Some of those in the Class photo include Robert Francis, Donald Shale, Fred Walters, Joseph Shaffer, Jess Kisabeth, Charlie Stultz, Louis Stagger, Charles Cover, N.N. Richards, Roy Hartley, Perry Smothers, Joy Shuman, Clark Richard, Tom Newell, Ray Youngblood, Frank Kimes, Eddie Mall, Everet Smith, Carl Muir, Park Richards, Tom Duffy, C.A. Eger, Harry Richards, W.R. Sprague, Paul Shaffer, Elmer Harris, Henry Eger, W.J. Rainey, Ray Clark, "Dad" Kelly, Oscar Rafferty, Wesley Keiser, Jess Brown, Ray Blinn, Sam Winterhalter, Charles Babb, James Gise, Walker Hartsook, Carl Lindsey, Ernest Weisinger, Earl Berry, C.H. Footit, Rev. E.C. Miley, Clark Richards, Juanita Sprague, A.R. Keiser, and C.W. Springer.

Looking south on Main Street from the corner of Main and North, the building in the foreground on the left is the Botto Block, built in 1905 by Louis Botto of Fostoria and Mr. Lavagi of Tiffin. The F.W. Woolworth store came to Fostoria in 1916 and took a 99-year lease on the first floor of the Botto Block. The second floor contained office space occupied by lawyers, doctors, dentists, realtors, and other professions. The third floor was a large hall, used mainly for dances.

The building next to it is the Cadwallader Block, which was built in 1907. From its inception, it was used exclusively by dry goods merchants for 67 years. These included the A. Weaver & Sons Company in 1907 and Kiebel & Wilson around 1915, which became the Wilson Dry Goods Company about 1919. Beckett & Ahlenius took over that location in 1923, which then became H.O. Ahlenius Company until 1974, when the Ahlenius Company quit business.

In the center of the photo, readers will recognize the old Colonial Theatre, and its marquee, later known as the State Theatre.

At the right of the photo, the top floor of the building at the southwest corner of Main and North was once a business college, which started after the Fostoria Academy burned. The second floor was office space. The first floor was occupied for the longest time by the A. Beesch Store, dealers in coffee, spices, dinnerware, and other household items. In later years, Ohio Savings and Loan occupied the first floor.

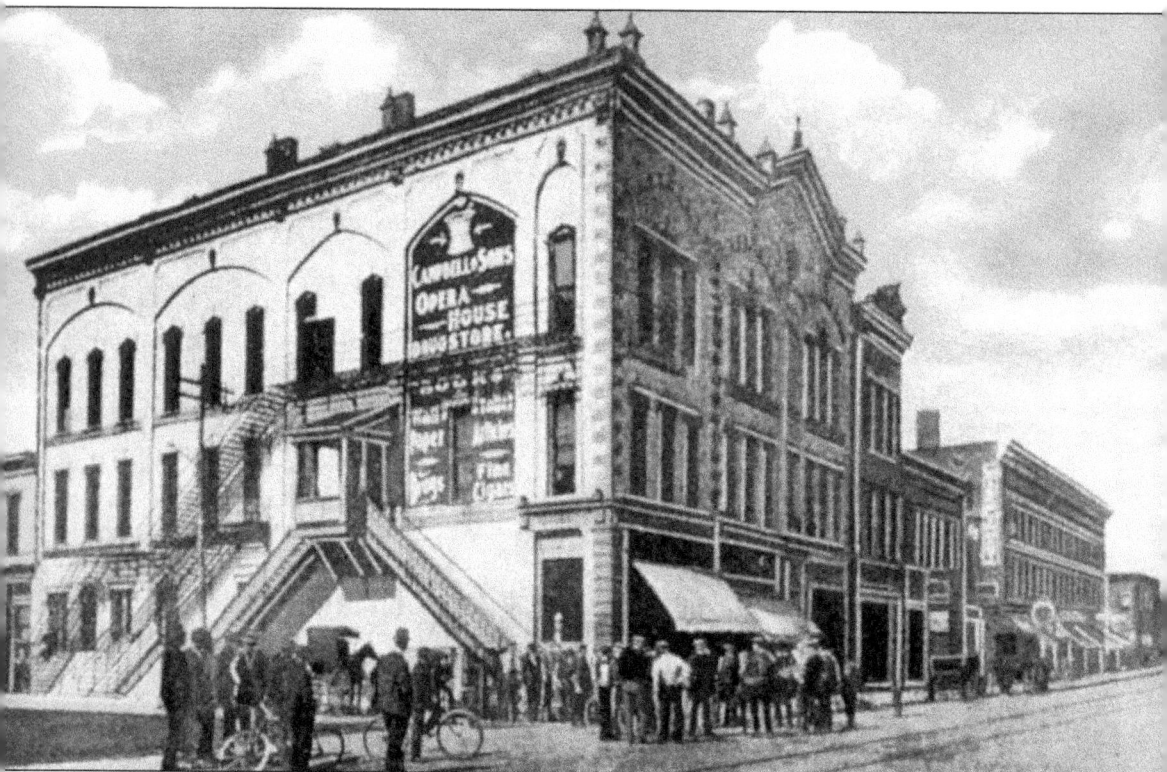

At the northwest corner of Main and Center looking north on Main Street is the Andes Block, the most imposing building on the block, named after the original owner who had it built; and the grandfather of Gladys (Andes) Harrison. The entire third floor of that building was once Fostoria's popular Opera House. In later years, stage and seats were removed and it was used for meetings and dancing. The second floor was the first location of Ohio Saving and Loan, and otherwise was filled with professional offices. First floor rooms housed many well-known merchants. The corner room was always the location of a drug store, the last being Edison's. Next to it there was always a men's clothing store, three of them being Mickey's, Lamfrom's, and Gary Weimerskirch's. Kleinhen Office Supply occupied a room in the block for many years.

A Mr. Quinlin, who conducted a bakery on the first floor and lived on the second floor, built the 2-story building midway between North and Center, known as the Quinlin Block, where the Smoke House poolroom is now. In the basement under the Smoke House there was once a bowling alley, operated by Harry Aldrich.

Here is a view looking north on Main Street from the corner of Main and Center. The 3-story building on the right was called the First National Bank Building, also the Emerine Building. It was built in 1892 and was considered to be the best built building on Main Street. The bank occupied the corner location on the first floor and was founded by Alonzo Emerine, a self-made man who started in business as a harness maker, and father of Andrew, who succeeded him as head of the bank. Other businesses on the ground floor just north of the bank included Mogles Restaurant and Snub Cummins Clothing Store for men. The second floor was filled with offices for doctors, dentists, and others. The third floor was headquarters for the Knights of Pithias Lodge. The First National Bank moved from the Emerine Building into the former Union National Bank building at Main and Tiffin Streets in 1933, where Tri-County is today. In 1948, the Emerine Building was demolished. Built of quarried Indiana sandstone, the Emerine Building was so sturdily constructed that the demolition team had a difficult time dismantling it. It was replaced by a new building for the S.S. Kresge Company.

South Main St. and Interurban Station, Fostoria, Oh

Here is a view looking south on Main Street from the corner of Main and Center in the early 1900s. The imposing building in the left of the photo (the southeast corner of Main and Center) is the Alcott Block, one of Fostoria's finest buildings. It was built by Captain Roger Alcott in 1893 and was the home to numerous businesses and professionals. The third floor was used by several lodges and also for wrestling matches.

To the south of the Alcott Block was the Hays Hotel. There were many hotels in Fostoria in the late 1800s and early 1900s, but the Hays House was the oldest and the most famous. The next-door (just south) Interurban Station, with electric trolley cars, brought traveling men from Tiffin, Findlay, Toledo, and Fremont, with connections for Cleveland, Detroit, Columbus, Lima, and other cities. The Hays House had a bar, barbershop, and dining room, which was also used by all of Fostoria's service clubs for their weekly dinner meetings. A large fire destroyed the Alcott Block and the Hays Hotel in 1962.

24

Here is a view looking north on Main Street from the corner of Tiffin and Main, *c.* 1900.

Shown here looking south on the east side of Main Street from Tiffin was the Foster Block. The Commercial Bank occupied the first floor corner.

Here is a view looking south on Main Street, with the west side of the street pictured, from Main and Center, c. 1923.

Shown here is a view looking north on Main Street from the corner of Main and South. The right side (northeast corner) was Mogles Restaurant, now Dell's. Fruth Hardware was just north, then Firestone and the J.C. Penney store.

Seen here is Foster Park, where the Municipal Building now stands. Prior to erecting the Municipal Building it was used for band concerts and ice cream socials. And prior to that it was the Foster property complex, where the C.W. Foster home stood along with the Governor Charles Foster home.

This photo shows the Security Building at the northwest corner of Main and South in the early 1900s. When built, it was claimed to be the strongest and most secure building in town, thus its name. Many will remember it as the home of Montgomery Ward.

Two

OUR HISTORIC HOMES

(In 1978 the Fostoria Antique Study Club revealed their program to award plaques to those residents of this community who own homes that meet their standards for Heritage Homes. After months of study they selected 12 homes and awarded and placed plaques on them. At the request of the editor of the *Review Times*, in-depth stories about the Heritage Homes initially selected by the Fostoria's Antique Study Club appeared in the "Potluck" column. We have selected some of these for inclusion in this book.)

BROWN HOME
(May 19 and 26, 1983)

The Brown home at 243 West Tiffin Street has been there about 118 years. Presently, the property is owned by Winston Underwood, where offices for his certified public accounting business are located. William McKinley, who became the 24th president of the United States, made a speech from the front porch of the house when he was seeking the office.

The house was acquired by Owen T. Brown in 1880, having arrived in Fostoria in 1875, at age 40. Upon arriving in Fostoria, he became a partner in Foster, Olmsted & Company. Charles Foster became governor of Ohio and secretary of the U.S. Treasury. Brown, in July of 1899, became president of the Mechanics Banking Company. He served three terms as a member of the City Council and president of the board when the city waterworks was built and contracts for city paving were given. Brown was a Republican, a member of the Masonic fraternity and the Presbyterian Church, serving as a trustee for 36 years. Owen T. Brown and his wife both died in Fostoria and are buried in Fountain Cemetery.

Wilbur Charles Brown, the son of Owen T. Brown, graduated from Fostoria High School in 1880 with highest honors. In April 1882, he entered the banking house of the Honorable Charles Foster in Fostoria. Foster was governor then and W.C. Brown's association with the bank continued until he became treasurer and general financial manager of the Harter Milling Co., Fostoria, which was the largest winter-wheat milling plant in the United States. The Harter Milling Co. later became today's Mennel Milling Company. Brown then became associated with the Honorable Abner McKinley, brother of President William McKinley, and immediately moved to New York City, where he rapidly became involved in various financial endeavors. He was one of the syndicate of capitalists who built the Detroit and Northern Railroad. In Fostoria, he organized the Fostoria Shade and Lamp Company, which at that time was one of the largest of its kind in the United States. From 1892–96 he was an aid to William McKinley, the Governor of Ohio.

Shown here is the Brown house at 243 West Tiffin Street, built 1863–1865.

CROCKER HOME
(March 26, 1981)

The Crocker home at 133 South Street, midway between Main and Poplar, on the south side, is more than 100 years old—with full basement, five main rooms on the first floor, plus bath and pantry, six main rooms on the second floor, including an area with a nursery and 2-room servant's quarters, and complete bath, an attic, all floored, well-lighted by windows and easily accessible!

In 1832, Roswell Crocker laid out the village of Rome. In 1830, John Crocker possessed the land, and after passing among other members of the Crocker family, it was owned by Roswell. The house that stands there today was built sometime between 1855 and 1861, making it at least 120 years old. The house stayed in the Crocker family until about 1940, when it was purchased by Blaine Hummel, who lived there until the time Daniel Wolph purchased it about two years ago.

The large front porch, a must for homes built in that era, protects the two front entrances—one on each side. It was probably used for a lot of "sitting" in the summer, back when the Crocker's lived there. The main entrance at the left is seldom used, primarily because it's more natural to approach the one on the right, straight ahead from the porch steps. The main entry on the left accommodates the front stairway to the second floor. The fireplace, facing the stairway, is of Italianate design, with light green ceramic tile on the front. The mantle is cherry, matching the rest of the room.

The stained-glass windows in the entry hall are just two of the many, which add to the charm of the house. The door for the main entry hall is 2 1/2 inches thick, all in cherry, with beveled plate glass. The floor in the entry hall is oak, finished light, combined with walnut, and laid in a parquet pattern. In the living room and dining room the floor is oak, finished light and laid in a vaulted pattern, which means that the laying started in the center of the room and progressed toward all four sides.

Shown here is the Crocker home at 133 South Street.

EGER HOME
(August 23, 1979)

Seventy-three years is a long time to live in one house. That's how long Miss Vera Eger has lived in the house at 504 McDougal Street, which was named a Heritage House by the Fostoria Antique Study Club. Miss Eger's parents, Charles and Lucy Eger, and brother Dean and sister Carrie, moved to Fostoria from Pleasant Bend, Ohio, in 1906 and took up residence in the house. The land on which the house was built was sold to Hanna Boyer in 1838 by the United States Government when Andrew Jackson was president. Boyer sold to Elizabeth Fisher in 1846; the Fishers sold to Melinda and W.H. Bush in 1861; the Bushes sold to John Walding, a local tailor, and he built the house in 1867, making it 112 years old. Walding lived there until 1902, and then sold the property to John Shiebel, and it was from him that the Egers bought it in 1906.

Miss Eger remembers that when they moved to McDougal Street, there was one big apple orchard that extended from their house, at the corner of Caples, eastward to Town Street, and southward there were just fields, no houses. She remembers that circuses and carnivals "set up" on the fields at what is now East Center and Tiffin Streets. Dean, her brother, carried water for the circus elephants to earn tickets for himself and Vera.

The Eger property is the same as it was when built, except for new roofs and paint jobs. It has been well- maintained and contains the charm of old houses of that era. It is a frame house, setting on a fieldstone foundation. The hot-air central heating system was built with the house. Unlike most coal-fired furnaces, it was enclosed with bricks, and looked more like a kiln, according to Miss Eger, who remembers it well. In later years it was dismantled and a gas-fired furnace installed.

Like most houses then, illumination was by kerosene lamps. Later, when natural gas was plentiful, gaslights were installed. In about 1920, electric wiring was installed in the house for illumination and other electrical requirements. Two fireplaces provided a means for supplementary heating, one in the dining room and another in a downstairs bedroom.

A rarity exists in the Eger house, which was common years ago, but rarely seen now: a pitcher pump in an old-fashioned apron sink. The pump was disconnected from the well many years ago. It is a relic of by-gone days, which Miss Eger hesitated to part with. The clock on the shelf above the pump belonged to Vera's father's mother. It still runs, even though it's at least 150 years old. In fact, the house is full of relics and antiques, each one treasured, having been a part of the family for nearly 100 years or more. Some of the items belonged to Miss Eger's grandparents on both sides of the family. Some of the items were brought to Fostoria on a huckster wagon.

The downstairs of the house has six rooms and a pantry, or buttery as they were often called 100 years ago. The upstairs has three bedrooms and a trunk room. Among other items of interest in the kitchen are an antique drop-leaf kitchen table, which accommodates extra insert boards for expansion, antique kitchen chairs, and a cupboard. The antique bed in the downstairs bedroom was given to Vera's mother when she was 15 years old, making it over 100 years old. The quilt on the bed was made by Vera's mother with the "Flower Garden" pattern.

A treasured spot of the house is the unique latticed porch at the back of the house, which provides shelter from most storms, and makes an outdoor spot to snack, read, and relax. The bench on the porch was a Methodist Church pew, brought from Pleasant Bend, as was the hanging lantern. Near the back porch is a very large walnut tree, which Mr. Eger planted when they moved there. An arbor still supports a grape vine that was there when the Egers moved in.

After coming to Fostoria from Pleasant Bend, Ohio, part of the family support was derived from a large vegetable garden. Mr. Eger worked at the Carbon Company at one time, and also at Harter, now

Mennel Milling. But very few Fostorians know that Mr. Eger and his sons, Lewis and Henry, started a potato chip factory here in 1916. It was the first one in this area. The factory was on the Eger property on McDougal Street. According to Vera it was unlike the modern, mechanized potato chip factories of today. But, it turned out a quality product, and was successful for many years. Vera remembers kids of all ages coming to the chip factory to get the free broken rejects at the end of each day's production. Later, Vera's two older brothers, George and Lewis, started a potato chip and pretzel factory in Sandusky. They also made ice cream cones—the old-fashioned, cone-shaped ones. Vera Eger and her deceased sister, Carrie, were both schoolteachers for many years, and her brother, Dean, carved out a successful career with F.W. Woolworth Company (see page 108).

Seen here is the Eger home at 504 McDougal Street.

FOSTER HOME
(October 18, 1979)

The C.W. Foster Home on South Main Street occupied the site of the present municipal building. The *Fostoria Daily Review* occupied the old home for a number of years. I have fond memories of the house and the grounds surrounding it, and the people who worked at the *Review* because that is where I got my start, as a boy in the business world. The Foster house was the home of C.W. Foster, father of Charles "Calico" Foster, who later became governor of Ohio and still later secretary of the U.S. Treasury.

The *Review* started out as the *Fostoria News* in 1860, as a weekly. In 1876, O.J. and J.P. De Wolfe acquired the paper. Later H.J. Lockhart became managing editor and John, his son, news editor. About that time it became a daily. In 1907, the old Foster house was leased, the Foster family having passed away, and the newspaper moved in from the previous location on West Tiffin Street. Reorganization resulted in John Lockhart becoming managing editor and holder of controlling interest. In 1913, F.M. Hopkins purchased Lockhart's interest in the paper. Later John Lockhart became editor of the *Times*. The Hopkins family came to Fostoria from Toledo, where he had editorial staff positions on the *Toledo News-Bee*, *Toledo Blade*, and *Toledo Times*.

My introduction to the newspaper and the Foster home was when I became a carrier boy in 1917, when Clayton Kinsey was circulation manager. In addition to carrying papers, I also helped Emma Reber in the mailroom. And, I won't forget working one summer in the basement foundry where the linotype metal was remelted daily and formed into ingots for reuse. It was a terrific job for a boy like me to undertake, being undersized and pretty lean. On Armistice Day 1919, I passed out an Extra Edition about the end of World War I, and took part in the celebration. The population went wild.

The old Foster home was quite a structure. Too bad it was demolished—it should have become Fostoria's number one historic site and museum, since the Foster family played such an important part in the town's early days. The double front doors of the Foster home led to the second floor editorial department via a beautiful staircase; or to the left, led into the business office, which was once the parlor of the Fosters.

When the *Review* acquired a larger and more adequate building in 1920 on East Center Street, where the *Review Times* is now, the Foster house was demolished, but the old front entry staircase was salvaged and installed in the Bill Daub home at 836 North Union Street, where the Walter Fruths now reside.

I used the front stairs in the old house many times later, when Art Murray worked in the editorial department for a year, starting in 1920. Art took an interest in me, as a newspaper carrier, and hired me to assist him collect news in the business district, paying me out of his own pocket the large sum of $2 per week. After soliciting the news items, Art taught me how to organize them into paragraphs, and type them on one of the old typewriters.

Looking at the accompanying photo of the Foster home, the reader will locate the editorial room by looking at the first group of windows on the right of the second floor. The room was undoubtedly a bedroom when the Fosters lived there. There was plenty of space on the second floor, where the Review Band practiced. Emma Reber, the longest continually employed individual at the *Review* and eventually the *Review Times*, had her mail room and bindery department on the second floor, reached by a back stairs or a hallway from the front stairs. If my memory serves me correctly, there were four large upstairs rooms.

Shown here is the C.W. Foster home, where the *Fostoria Review* once was published.

Members of the Review Band of World War I days shown here, from left to right, are as follows: (front row) William Swartz, unknown, Jack Wetherall, Harry Thurber Jr., Harry Thurber Sr. (director), unknown, George Burkhart, and Clyde Gregory; (back row) Boday, Lou Lambright, unknown, unknown, Russell Groves, unknown, unknown, Ross Overmire, unknown, and unknown.

HARRISON HOME

(June 17, 1982)

The Harrison house was built in the late 1840s or early 50s. It may be the oldest house on West Tiffin Street. It was Italianate architecture, with Mansard roof campanile and balcony areas. The balcony railing was of decoratively carved wood. During Mr. Harrison's ownership, the wood railing, which had deteriorated, was replaced by wrought iron. The Seneca Lumber Company had the tooling to duplicate the original but the cost would have been prohibitive. The house next to it was built later to be used as servants quarters.

Your author believes that the photo was taken in the late 1890s or early 1900s, at which time the house was owned by Mr. and Mrs. John Ebersole. My wife said one of the ladies in the photo was her grandmother, Hattie Drenner, sister of John Ebersole. John Ebersole is probably standing on the balcony.

Exclusive of the basement, the house is four stories high. The two top stories could logically be called "lookouts," and that may be exactly what they were used for back at the time of construction. The day Harrison took me on a tour of the house, we climbed the narrow, steep stairs which lead from the second floor to the highest point in the structure. In both of the two top levels, I could see in all directions. Whoever built and owned the house originally must have been at least moderately wealthy and probably owned farmland south of the village of Rome. The first floor of the house has six rooms; the second floor has four rooms.

Who the owners or residents of the house may have been in the earliest days is unknown, but it is known that J.F. Richart resided there in 1893, followed by John P. Ebersole from 1899. Charles W. Fox, who owned and farmed land south of town, was owner of the property from 1915 until Harrison became the possessor.

The Harrison house has, in your author's view, the most unusual appearance of any in town. It was originally well-constructed and has stood the test of time. The present owner has preserved it through good maintenance and it is not only a credit to early period design and construction, but worthy of being selected as a Heritage House by the Antique Study Club.

Shown here is Floyd Harrison's Heritage House at 215 West Tiffin Street.

HALSEY HOME
(June 7, 1979)

Like other Fostorians, I have travelled past the Robert Halsey home at 1004 North Union Street many times and admired the outward appearance—often wondering what it looked like inside. I telephoned Mrs. Halsey to arrange an interview. Stepping into the home I was immediately impressed with the spaciousness and charm of this well-maintained old house, at least 100 years old, which qualifies it for consideration as a Heritage Home in Fostoria, as selected and named by the Antique Study Club.

Like most old deeds for properties in Fostoria, the initial entry indicates first ownership of the land by John Gorsuch, having been sold to him by the United States Government in 1832; the official papers carrying the name of President Andrew Jackson and Elijah Haywood, Commissioner of the General Land Office. Originally, the land that Gorsuch purchased from the government consisted of 88 acres. Later, he bought additional land adjacent to the original purchase, making a total of 177 acres, which he and his wife sold to R.F. Caples. The Caples came from New Philadelphia to Seneca County in 1815. There are many other Caples in Seneca County history and the land was sold and resold many times within the Caples family.

In 1864, Philip and Sarah Caples sold the property to Benjamin Leonard for a consideration of $11,000, the first sizeable dollar figure to be entered in any of the deed transactions. It was then part of the Leonard addition, and the house at 1004 North Union Street was built on inlot 650 and part of inlot 659. The lot upon which the Halsey house sets is 100-by-200 feet, which well-suits this large 2-story brick house, with Italian type architecture of the Victorian era and ornate roof brackets and trim. The foundation is made of round, smooth field stone, of which there was plentiful quantities then, as now. Like most old houses built 100 years ago or more, the house is supported on large, square, hand-hewn native timbers from the forests in this area.

Stepping into the front entrance of the house I stood and gazed—fascinated with the circular stairway that leads to the second floor. The staircase is made of ash and oak—quite ornate and finished naturally. The walls in the entry hall and up the stairway are papered with an appropriate medallion pattern. A beautiful antique kerosene chandelier at the foot of the stairs once lighted that area, but in more recent years the fixture has been electrified.

The living room is approximately 26-by-32 feet, with 10 1/2-foot ceiling, as are all the downstairs rooms. Originally, the present living room was two rooms—the one end being a small room for study or bedroom. The present mantel, which replaced the original fireplace, was installed in more recent years when the Richard Collins family occupied the house. The original chimney is still utilized for the mantel.

The many pieces of antique furniture, which the Halseys have inherited or collected, find a natural setting in this old house, and reminded me of colonial and southern homes that have become showplaces in this country. One such piece is the slant-front secretary, made of black walnut, which is in the Halsey living room. Another item is the three-corner oak cupboard, a family heirloom, which may have been made by a member of Mrs. Halsey's family. A prize piece of furniture in the Halsey dining room is the walnut cabinet that the Collins left in the basement because no one wanted it—probably because it was covered with green paint. Now completely refinished as natural wood it has regained its original charm and status for the old house.

When the Collins lived in the house they modernized the kitchen area, putting in all new cabinets and converting the old pantry to a downstairs bath. The Halseys have since brought the cabinet fronts up-to-date with new doors. A back stairway leads to the second floor and provides a quick way up or down—especially for the Halsey children. The upstairs consists of three bedrooms and a bath.

The front and back porches are typical of those that were usually built on houses of that era. The back porch, which was rebuilt by the Halseys, is a treasured spot for outdoor gatherings, since it is partially secluded and looks out on the well-kept lawn, flower garden, and play area.

KIMES HOME
(January 25, 1979)

Sometime around 1835, it is believed, Dr. Marcus Dana established residence in the house that was built for him in Risdon, on ground that is adjacent to land now marked as the original square of that village, at the northwest corner of Countyline and Summit Streets. The land was part of the acreage that pioneer land developer John Gorsuch owned, having purchased it at a very low price from the United States Government, and finalized by papers signed by President Andrew Jackson. Gorsuch sold the land to Dr. Dana in 1832. Dr. Dana was a graduate of the Philadelphia Medical College and practiced medicine in Risdon/Fostoria from 1834 until his death in 1853.

The original plot of ground for the house was 66-by-99 feet. Later, Dr. Dana purchased from John Becker the corner lot, bordering on Summit Street, and then making the property 132-by-99 feet. The 132 feet extended north from what is now Summit Street, and the 99 feet west from Countyline Street. Dana's original house was only part of the house as it now exists, occupied by Mr. and Mrs. Elwood Kimes. The first building was the portion at the left shown in the photo. Excluding the front porch with the overhang and the wood pillars, the dimensions of the house were 20 1/2-by-30 1/2 feet.

The house was entered by the same front door that was hung there at least 145 years ago. The original lock on the front door is still there. Entry was into a large room 19-by-19 feet, which must have served as living room, dining room, and kitchen, since that room contained the only chimney for the house. Ceilings were 10 1/2 feet high. Walls were plastered, and flooring was 6-inch-wide boards. Wood from the native forests that surrounded Fostoria provided the timbers, siding, flooring, shingles, and interior wood-trim for the house. The original wood siding is still intact. The pioneer settlers of that day were skilled in working with wood, including the carvings that adorned the interior. Back of the living area were two bedrooms, each 9 1/2-by-15 feet. The partition between the bedrooms was removed by the Kimes—making it one large room.

The ornate, original oil lighting fixture that illuminated the living area still hangs from the ceiling where it was installed. However, in recent years the Kimes had it electrified. The fixture originally could be lowered and raised to facilitate the filling of the three oil lamps that furnished illumination.

The foundation is brick, which has often raised questions by some who say, "Where did the bricks come from back then?" According to Elwood Kimes, his father related years ago that there was a vein of clay west of the house, near the creek, where there was a small brick-making plant. Only one large 12-inch square, wood-hewn beam is used under the house for support—the rest of the supports are wood logs, approximately 12 inches in diameter, not squared, but just as they were cut from the forest.

In later years, an addition was built into the north side of the house. The addition 24 1/2-by-30 1/2 feet added approximately 746 square-feet of living quarters to accommodate the Dana family. The addition was probably added somewhere around 1850, according to the Kimeses.

Mr. and Mrs. Howard Kimes, father and mother of Elwood, present owner, acquired the house in 1908, seven years after he moved into it as a tenant. He was 25 years of age then, having been born in 1876. In later years, Mr. Kimes built an upstairs to the addition that had been added to the north side of the house by Dana, thus providing two more bedrooms.

Other changes to the house include excavation for basement and furnace; fireplace built in the original part of the house, tapped in to the original chimney; tile ceilings installed in the living and bedroom of original part, to provide insulation, since no attic existed; and modernized kitchen. A garage has been built just south of the original structure. East of the garage there once stood a 1-story frame building approximately 20-by-20 feet, which served as a station house for the stage coaches serving Risdon.

Seen here is the Halsey Heritage Home at 1004 North Union Street.

The Kimes house is shown as it stands today at the northwest corner of Summit and Countyline Streets.

Three

OUR BUSINESS
AND INDUSTRY

(CONTINUED FROM VOLUME ONE)

COMMERCIAL BANK
(July 6 and 13, 1978)

This year is the 75th anniversary of the Commercial Bank and Savings Company here in Fostoria. At its 50-year point, the bank published its annual statement; also a brief history of the bank's founding, and first officers, from which I quote:

> In 1902, a group of prominent businessmen and farmers in this community, with an abiding faith in the future of Fostoria, and being convinced that a real need existed for another sound and progressive bank   to serve the people of this area, organized the third financial institution of this city, The Commercial   Bank and Savings Company. A charter was issued by the State of Ohio on October 23, 1902, and on   November 5, 1902, the organization was completed by the election of directors: E.J. Cunningham,   Charles Ash, W.H. Jones, John E. Finsel, R.D. Sneath, N. Saltsman, C. German, Theo Wentz, John Noble. Officers elected were President, E.J. Cunningham; V. President, Charles Ash; Cashier, J.D. McDonel; and Asst. Cashier, Charles Gribble.

The new bank was capitalized for $50,000 and a surplus of $10,000: small sums in comparison with the figures today. By the end of the first year of operation the bank reported total resources of $325,896, while individual deposits stood at $251,827.

The only living employee of the early years is Roy Hoffman, who joined the bank as bookkeeper in 1911. "Banking practices were far different then as compared to today," according to Hoffman. "We had one hand-operated adding machine . . . bookkeeping was all done by hand . . . no computers then." I asked Hoffman what was the most important event he remembered in his 45 years with the bank. He reflected only briefly, and then said, "the bank holiday in 1930. First of all I had to make a complete list of all our customers with savings and checking accounts and certificates. I don't remember the exact figures, but they were permitted to draw a percentage of their money." Hoffman said there was no great "run" on the bank and no customer ever lost a penny of their money.

By 1912, the bank officers saw the need to remodel and refurbish. A large balcony was built over the main floor at the rear. After the remodeling was completed an open house was held which attracted 2000 to 3000 people, according to the newspaper report. Anderson's seven-piece orchestra, on the balcony, furnished music. Miss Clara Tunstill (now deceased), who later became Mrs. Richard Kelly, and Miss Lenore McDonel handed out souvenirs—carnations to the ladies and cigars to the men.

At the time of the open house, 1915, the bank reported capital, deposits, and surplus stood at $700,000. By the time of World War I, 1918, total resources of the bank stood at $1,112,418. At the end of 25 years, 1928, the bank's total resources were $1,548,030. June 30, 1930, at the time of the bank holiday, the bank showed total resources of $1,447,298.

In 1932, Lucian E. Kinn was named the bank's third president. With his vast business experience, he brought new vigor to the Bank. By 1945, the assets had climbed to $3,840,344. At the time of his death, the bank had grown considerably, with total assets of $6,347,601 and deposits of $5,949,828.

With the passing of Lucian Kinn, John Gutknecht became the bank's new president in 1952. During his presidency, the bank built the new main office on Perry Street; remodeled the original location to serve as the downtown branch; established a branch in Bascom; and merged into itself the New Riegel State Bank. And the assets continued to grow from approximately $6,347,000 in 1962 to $27,000,000 in 1974. In 1974, Frank J. Kinn, the son of former president Lucian Kinn, was named president and chief executive officer.

A number of women have made significant contributions to the bank, including Cara (Latshaw) Davis, Carmel Huth, Anna Rose Nichols, and Celia (Dicken) Cadwallader.

Shown here is the Commercial Bank at the corner of Main and Tiffin Streets, 1930.

Here is an interior view of the bank. Pictured inside the early Commercial Bank are, from left to right, Tony Welly, Harris Zimmerman, and Charles Yost. The inset is of Roy Hoffman, who was standing in the original photo that was damaged by age.

DAIRIES
(May 17 and 24, 1979, and October 6, 1983)

This is the story about milk—one of life's precious commodities dating back to the earliest history of man, and down to the past and present dairy business here in Fostoria. As far back as 9,000 B.C., cow's milk is mentioned in history. Milk and its by-products are mentioned 44 times in the Old Testament of the Bible. Excavations in Switzerland indicate that the people there made cheese as early as 4,000 B.C. The first importation of cattle to the colonies was in 1611, to Jamestown, Virginia.

It was not until 1878 that milk was delivered in bottles, introduced in New York City. Before the advent of the glass bottle, milk was sold from unsealed containers; the buyer furnishing his own container, the milk being dipped out in whatever quantity was purchased. Your writer remembers very vividly, as a young child of perhaps five, the milk wagon stopping at our house. Mother had a tin pail with a lid that held approximately one half gallon, which was our milk container for receiving the milk. The wagon had a foot-operated bell, which announced their presence in the neighborhood. The purveyor to our house probably was either E.W. Kipka or O.E. Kipka, brothers who both started in the dairy business in Fostoria in 1896.

The first dairy establishment in Fostoria was the Morning Glory Creamery, located on South Main at Jones, in 1889. In 1919, three of Fostoria's larger dairies and creameries started. Fostoria Union Dairy was one of those starting in 1919. Union Dairy continued in business until 1957, at which time it was sold to a company in Toledo.

Ammer Dairy Company, also started in 1919, and was located on East Center Street where the *Review Times* parking lot is now. They were in business until 1922, when Seneca Dairy Company took over the business. Fostoria Creamery, the third dairy started in 1919, was located in the vacated, dilapidated building still standing on South Union Street beside the B&O tracks. They later became known as George Freese and Son Creamery. They did not sell milk retail, but turned all of their milk into butter and other products selling wholesale.

Fox Dairy was started in 1929 by Elias Fox, who milked a few cows, bottled the milk and distributed it to customers from the trunk of his car. Later his son Al joined the operation and it grew to a larger operation, providing pasteurized milk, cottage cheese, coffee cream, whipping cream, and chocolate milk. They were in business until 1962, when they sold out to San-a-Pure, from Findlay, who continued to serve Fostoria with home delivery until a few years ago, when the declining number of customers who wanted that service made it impractical.

Ziegler Bros. Dairy also made ice cream and ran a retail ice cream shop in the frame building that stood on North Main Street, now demolished, where Kinn and Theobald Insurance office is now. Russell Dairy never operated a milk processing plant, but purchased their product from Fox Dairy, packaged under the Russell name.

There have been 19 dairies in Fostoria, including the following: E.W. Kipka, Dillon Dairy, Co-op Milk Assn., Linwood Dairy, O, E. Kipka, Fox Dairy, Zeigler Bros. Dairy, Holman's Dairy, Weavers Dairy, Ohio Farmers, Sen-Wood Dairy, Babcock Dairy, Welly Dairy, C.H. Shoemaker, Sah's Dairy, G.H. Russell, O.D. Wells, Ward Dairy, and K.K.C.

The dairies depended on farmers in this area for their supply of milk and cream, it being brought to town by horse and wagon or by railroad. The dairies all delivered their products by horse-drawn wagons. These horses knew their routes as well as the drivers and could be trusted to stop at each customer's house and turn corners without directions.

Posing here are the Union Dairy employees, 1923. They are, from left to right, J.R. Reeves, Charles Stoy, C.E. Young, Vera (Earl) Stoneberger, Howard Newell, Ott Crow, Ernie Medley, unknown, Carl Myers, Bill Catlett, George Kuhn, and William Kimball.

Here is an O.E. Kipka milk wagon. He called his business Lynwood Dairy.

Delivery Services
(February 22, 1979)

Back approximately 70 years ago, Fostoria had a service which provided delivery of merchandise from most of this city's merchants. It was a valuable service from the standpoint of the merchants as well as the public. Each merchant did not need to maintain separate service, and the cost was less for them. Consumers then were in the era when automobiles were not yet a common conveyance. Imagine lugging home a 25-pound sack of flour, plus other food items, which might fill a couple of bags—but without bags. Back then, if you went to the grocery you had a couple of market baskets.

The Union Delivery service existed in Fostoria around 1910, maybe a little earlier. They had seven wagons that made up the fleet, with seven trusty horses that needed no occasional "overhauls"—just food, water, brushing, and currying. When this photo was taken the "rigs" were lined up beside the Poley Building on Perry Street. The man in the photo wearing a complete suit (fourth from right) was N.B. Flack, owner of Union Delivery.

In later years, the delivery service was called Merchants Delivery, after the local merchants took it over as a joint enterprise, with Duane Gear as manager. That was around 1918, according to Henry Gary, who worked there at that time. He also recalls that the delivery schedules were two each morning and afternoon. Each wagon had a territory to cover. Some Fostorians will also remember that the service went under the name of Central Delivery at one time, when "Spot" Rohrs owned it. Other people who worked for the delivery service at some time, as recalled by Gary, were Forest Crow, Archie Crow, "Peg" Clary, Wendel Morel, Clarence Waldron, and Gene Jordan.

Union Delivery Service comprised seven wagons.

First National Bank
Dillinger Robbery

(January 15 and 22, 1981)

May 3, 1934, was the important day in Fostoria when the notorious John Dillinger gang came to town and left with $17,299 after robbing the First National Bank. The gang left vivid memories for many—just citizens and bystanders, the police who were unable to injure, capture, or deter the robbers—but most importantly, bank employees Bill Daub and Ruth Harris, who were used as hostages to make their getaway.

Fostoria had been considered practically 100 percent safe from bank robbery with more than 140 trains passing through town, which would serve as a deterrent against a hasty escape. But, the Dillinger gang had planned their robbery carefully, had studied the town's physical layout and the railroad situation, and knew that they had to escape in a northwesterly direction, the only area of town where there were no railroad tracks to deter them.

The robbery took place at about 2:30 p.m. Two men, both in their early 30s or 40s entered the Orwig Drug Store, where Ralph Orwig and Bert Miller were talking, and then went into the lobby of the bank. The two men had overcoats over their arms, concealing their submachine guns and muslin sacks to hold their loot. "Stick 'em up" were the only words spoken by the pair as they entered the bank. Frances Billyard had just left her teller's window when the bandits entered. She slipped through the door behind them and notified Police Chief Frank Culp that the robbery was in progress. Culp, with patrolman Louis Stagger, ran into the O.C. Harding Jewelry Store on the north side of the bank lobby and attempted to enter the lobby, but the robbers saw them and opened fire as they tried to get into the elevator. Culp had always said the elevator was a perfect place to be in case of a robbery. The elevator had been moved to the second floor by the attendant Evelyn Anderson, so Culp and Stagger were in the open. They returned fire, but Culp was hit. The two dashed into the jewelry store where Culp collapsed in a chair, but ordered Stagger "to go to the station for a riot gun." The chief told firefighters Charles Wise and Art Shuck, also present, to "get some help." The two tried to shoot back at the bandits but were unable to get a bead on them. Inside the bank building, 45 to 50 shots were fired. Cashier R.W. Powley was hit in the back by a bullet, which struck a suspender buckle and was partially deflected; however, his wound was about one inch deep. Culp sustained the most serious wound of any of those who were hit. The bullet that struck him entered one lung and crushed a rib. Robert Sheilds, another bystander, was hit in the foot. All were taken to Fostoria City Hospital.

While the bandits inside were scooping up the money in their sacks, the rest of the gang on the outside were making it unpleasant and dangerous for anyone to thwart their escape by keeping up a steady fire in all directions. Floyd Kelly, owner of Kelly's Hot Dog Stand, heard the bullet fire and opened his door in time to see Mayor George Cameron run into the Ohio Hotel to telephone the State Patrol office in Findlay. William Sendelbach, who resided at 623 Cherry Street, escaped injury by a narrow margin when a bullet passed through his pant leg. Harold Peters was standing at the window of a store when a bullet plowed into a wall near him. Miss Peg Ingram, who thought she was safe in the R.C. Guernsey's law office, just missed being hit by a sub-machine gun bullet. Florence Altweis, who was a secretary in Mayor Cameron's office, stepped away from the door just a moment before two bullets whizzed through. Roscoe Carle, publisher of the *Fostoria Times*, who had been standing across the street in front of the Ohio Savings & Loan, moved just before two bullets shattered the window glass where he had been. Dr. Pelton, in his dental office above the Commercial Bank, had stray bullets come through his office windows, where he was working on a patient.

The writer of this column was an employee of the *Fostoria Review* at that time, and as soon as word reached the office of the robbery in progress, I ran to the corner. The sound of bullets hitting the buildings or ricocheting off prompted me to beat a hasty retreat back to the office.

As the Dillinger gang finished scooping up the bank's money and were ready to exit, one of the bandits was reported to have said, "It's too hot out there; lets go through the store's side door" on Tiffin Street where their escape car was parked. Dillinger ordered Bill Daub in the back seat, then changed his mind and told him to stand on the running board. Likewise, Van Meter ordered Ruth Harris to stand on the other running board and held her wrist tightly from his position in the back seat. The escape car roared west on Tiffin Street to Wood, turning north to Perry, then to Union, making its way out Perrysburg Road, at speeds of 70 miles per hour. They dumped roofing nails out of the back window to deter pursuers.

Later, it was reported by Harris, that she felt faint from the ordeal and wondered if she would ever get back home. Finally Daub said, "We're not of any further use to you, why don't you let us go?" "All right," one of the bandits said, "We'll slow down and you two jump off." As the car slowed to almost a stop, "jump" commanded the bandits, and then they roared off. The two hostages picked themselves up from the dusty road and started walking. A cattle truck finally picked them up and brought them to town. On the way a pursuit car passed them. The escape car was trailed to Stearns Corner, where it turned west and went across a field, then back on the road where the trail was lost. Harris and Daub were not physically injured, but probably suffered equally as much by shock. Daub's death later was attributed at least in part to the shock of the experience.

The bank holdup had some humorous anecdotes: Charlie Gribble, one of Fostoria's well known citizens back then, was well over 70 at that time, but he proved he could still move fast when necessary. He was in attorney John Gutknecht's office. They heard the shooting and went down to the mezzanine floor to see what was happening. They saw the holdup in progress and one of the bandits at that moment swung his machine gun up toward them, sending bullets through the window. Gribble and Gutknecht made a hasty retreat up the stairs, but John didn't pass Charlie until they nearly reached the top.

A.E. Mergenthaler, vice president of the bank, was at work at his desk on the mezzanine floor. He looked down to see what the commotion was all about. One of the bandits with a machine gun ordered him to come down. He replied, "No thanks," and returned to his desk.

The news of the robbery spread like wildfire throughout the community and the nearby towns. People flocked to Fostoria to see what had happened. It was almost like a holiday. Restaurants had an overflow of business the rest of that day and the next.

Dillinger was never a vicious killer, as opposed to some of his gang members. Many times he averted killings by members of the gang. Whenever his associates did kill during holdups, Dillinger was reported to have said, "Why did you do that?" Dillinger often bragged that he could rob a bank without harming anyone. He was always pleasant to the teller and cashiers when asking them to hand over all the money. Dillinger was paroled from Michigan City on May 22, 1933. One report said that the following Sunday he attended the Friend's Church back in Mooresville. The pastor Gertrude W. Reiner saw John sitting with his father and preached a sermon on the Prodigal Son. Throughout the service he sat and cried, later telling the preacher how much good the sermon had done him.

Two weeks later, it was reported that Dillinger was active in recruiting ex-cons for his gang. And the next year or so he gained the reputation of being the most spectacular bank robber in the United States and was on the FBI's list of the most wanted men. Dillinger was supposedly killed by FBI agents as he and his two girlfriends left the Biograph Theatre in Chicago on July 22, 1934.

Opposite, Top Photo: Pictured here is the First National Bank opening, 1934.

Insert: John Dillinger.

Opposite, Bottom Photo: Involved in the robbery, from the left and top to bottom, were the following: Andrew Emerine, Bank President; R.S. Powley, Cashier; Police Chief Frank Culp; Bill Daub, Assistant Cashier; Ralph Barbour, Bank Teller; George Cameron, Mayor; Robert Shields, bystander (shot); Ernie Duffield; Ed Walters, ex-policeman (shot).

FLOUR MILLS
(March 23, 1978)

Many older Fostorians will remember the Franke brothers: Charles, August, and James. Charles came to Fostoria in 1893, and with his brother, August, who had been with the Harter (milling) Company in this city a little over a year, opened a small retail flour and feed store in the Longfellow block on East North Street. They started with only $300 capital.

Back then, the housewife baked homemade bread, and made biscuits and cakes "from scratch." Also, in that era many people kept chickens and maybe some ducks, a cow or two, and maybe a horse—so they needed feed. Also, the farmers surrounding Fostoria came to town to buy feed for their herds of cattle, and horses, which they used for plowing.

By 1898, the Franke brothers, Charles and August, were operating a gristmill on East Tiffin Street near the Toledo and Ohio Central railroad tracks, which later was known as the New York Central, and still later Penn Central. In 1899, they purchased the old elevator that was located on North Main Street, previously owned by Dr. J.W. Smith of Pontiac, Michigan. The Franke brothers remodeled the old mill and installed new and modern machinery to operate an up-to-date flour mill, with a capacity of 125 barrels per day. They called it Fostoria City Mills. This is the mill where we purchased freshly ground whole wheat for our morning hot cereal when I was a boy.

In 1900, the two brothers built the Franke Block on North Main Street, now owned by George Pappas, in which his Candyland Restaurant is operated. In their new building the Franke brothers established their retail store for flour, feed, and grain. In about 1919 or 1920, Fostoria City Mills was sold to another local group and the name was changed to Fostoria Milling Company. They ceased to operate around 1921.

Today Fostoria is known for the Ohio Farmers Grain and Supply and the Mennel Milling Company.

Shown here are the Franke brothers' Fostoria City Mills.

Shown here are the Harter Flour Mills.

Shown here are Ohio Farmers grain silos (foreground) and the Mennel Milling Company (background).

FOUNDRIES
(September 20, 1979)

The several old foundries that existed in Fostoria in the last century can't be compared with the present day Chrysler Fostoria Foundry in terms of size, employment, and production volume. However, those that existed 100 years ago produced castings for a wide variety of products. Two of those castings were recently discovered.

When Gray Printing Company purchased and demolished the house at 328 East North Street to use the lot for parking, Clayton Risner, who was filling in the basement area, made several "finds." One of them was a cast iron part, which appeared to have been a part of a door for a stove or furnace. The part, and perhaps the rest of the casting, was manufactured by John Brothers, Fostoria. The name "John Bros." and "Fostoria Ohio" can still be seen in the casting, as well as a figure of a cherub. Although the part is definitely a casting and was manufactured here, no reference could be found in historical data for a foundry by that name in Fostoria.

At about the same time that part was found, Mrs. Greene, an employee at Buckeye Aluminum Extrusions and a "Potluck" reader, called to my attention a cast iron heating stove from the last century, still in existence at the home of one of her relatives, Harry Rogers, a retired farmer, living on South Prospect Street, Bloomville. It was manufactured at Fostoria Foundry and Machine Company. These two "finds" have prompted me to write this story about foundries during the earlier days of Fostoria.

As far as I can ascertain, the earliest foundry establishment in Fostoria was in 1860, owned by C.W. Bonnell and located at Perry and High Streets. The principal products were scrapers, plows, agriculture implements, vases, columns, and house castings. The company employed nine people and the value of the annual production was estimated at $15,000.

In 1880, the Fostoria Foundry & Machine Works was owned by Charles Foster, Nicholas Portz, and F. Manecke. It was an outgrowth of the foundry owned earlier by Bement & Robers, still earlier by Roberts & Company, and later C & B.W. Bonnell & Company. In 1885, a brass foundry at Titusville, Pennsylvania, was moved to Fostoria and consolidated with the Fostoria Foundry & Machine Works and became known as the Fostoria Brass & Bronze Manufacturing. This consolidated company manufactured a patented tapping machine, which was sold nationwide. It was located where the post office is now, at Center and Wood Streets.

Voglesson's Foundry, a small industry, was located in the western part of Fostoria during the earlier days, but I found no further reference to it in old historical notes.

In 1905, two Fostorians, N.G. Copley and a Mr. Shork, designed a water and steam pressure regulator system which came to be used extensively on hot water and steam generating systems. The product was used by utility companies, on steamships, by industry, and even at Boulder Dam. The complete line was described in their catalog as: "feed water regulators, pump governors, regulating valves, drainage controls, heater controls, and pressure regulators." The company to manufacture the devices later became known as S-C Regulator Company, the name being derived from the initials of the designers, Shork and Copley. At first they started in the old foundry building at Perry and High Streets. Later, they required more space and moved to the Gas Light Company building on East Crocker Street in 1923 or 1924.

The S-C Regulator had a competitor—the Swartout Company, Cleveland, which was having trouble competing with the quality of the local company's superior design. So, Swartout bought S-C Regulator in 1927 and moved it to their Orrville plant, where it continued to produce the regulators.

Pictured here is the Fostoria Foundry and Machine Company, also known as the Brass & Iron Works Company, at Wood and Center Streets.

Shown here is the S-C Regulator Mfg. on East Crocker Street.

GAS COMPANIES
(August 17, 1978)

There were once 12 glass plants in Fostoria. This glass era was closely related to the discovery of oil and gas in the area.

In 1886, the world-famed Carg gas well was struck this side of Findlay. It initially had flow of 20,000,000 cubic feet per day. It reportedly roared and burned with a flame over a hundred feet high that could be seen and heard over a radius of ten miles. For more than a year the Lake Erie and Western Railroad ran excursions from distances to see the marvelous sight. That event was the real beginning of glass industry in this area.

However, Fostoria had two glass factories a year before, since smaller gas strikes had been made earlier. All of the area from Bowling Green to Lima, including Bairdstown, Bloomdale, and North Baltimore became boom towns as the result of the oil and gas strikes, and they all suffered reversely when the wells stopped producing. Findlay was the center of production.

The Northwestern Ohio Natural Gas Company, with Governor Charles Foster as its president, was organized to finance the drilling of more wells and to lay a large gas main into town, into which industry could tap for FREE gas. $70,000 was raised for the project; soon the news was spread abroad, and attracted more glass factories to locate here. Some of the glass factories were organized by local people.

Gas was made available for home heating and lighting, and the cost was $1 per month. In later years when the supply dwindled, users found it undependable for winter use. I remember those days—and the switch we made to coal when winter arrived.

Gordon Gray, in a paper he wrote years ago, described the beauty of the gas street lights which were installed in Fostoria following the laying of the gas lines in the city: "In the early fall of 1888 when my mother brought my brother, Merton, and myself to this fairyland of Fostoria . . . the impression of the magic city upon my childhood brain was of lasting duration. Coming in on an early evening Nickel Plate, we were met at the train by my father who drove us through the streets of this illuminated, magic town of Fostoria. Street lights twinkled on every corner."

Older Fostorians, including your editor, remember those gaslights, which continued to light our streets until 1922. Likewise will we remember Angelo and Frank Di Cesare who, on bicycles, covered the city, morning and evening, lighting and extinguishing the lights. They were father and uncle, respectively, of Julie Di Cesare.

There came a time during the "gas-days" when it became evident that it was necessary to harness the precious fuel to enable local industry and residents to utilize it more effectively. According to Fostorian Edna Hatfield, in approximately 1888 the facilities for the City Heat and Light Company were built at the corner of Columbus Avenue and East Crocker Street. The large tank, shown in the accompanying photo, was used for storage of gas, and the large building housed facilities for pressurizing it.

By the turn of the century the Logan Natural Gas and Fuel Company had come into existence and was piping gas into Fostoria to supplement the dwindling supply of gas from local wells. For many years the local office for Logan Gas was in the room now occupied by Holden Coin Shop on East North Street in the Botto Building. Ed Leppard was the local manager of Logan Gas.

Gas lights on Main Street, 1885.

Seen here is the City Heat and Light Company at the corner of Columbus Avenue and East Crocker Street .

THE GLASS ERA
FACTORIES

(August 23, 1978)

Some years ago when I was doing considerable traveling for the Fostoria Pressed Steel Corp., and whenever fellow travelers or business people learned I was from Fostoria, they invariably would say, "Oh, that's where Fostoria glassware is made." They still associated the two names even thought the glassware is not made here anymore.

In the 1880s, when an abundance of gas in this area became known, and it was offered free to any industry that wanted to settle here, the glass industry instantly took advantage of the offer. It was a bonanza for them, since they needed large quantities of fuel to melt and fuse the basic ingredients—silicia, sand, soda ash, and limestone—that went into their products.

In no time the free offer attracted glass manufacturers from distant points, and also induced local interest to set-up factories. In 1887, the first of 12 glass factories started operating here. The accompanying map shows how glass factories were soon scattered all over the town. The following provides a condensed historical account of each. (The letter suffixes indicate locations in circles on the accompanying map, page 52)

THE FOSTORIA GLASS COMPANY (A).

Founded in 1887 around a nucleus of experienced glassmakers and workmen from eastern and southeastern Ohio, where the glass industry was already active. It was fostered by businessmen in Fostoria, including Charles Foster. The plant was located on South Vine Street where Seneca Wire is now. It manufactured a variety of tableware, which became famous—and the name Fostoria is still prestigious in the industry and among buyers of fine West Virginia, and continued to use the name "Fostoria."

THE SENECA GLASS COMPANY (A).

Immediately after the Fostoria Glass Company left this city, another group of glass makers organized the Seneca Glass Company and took over the plant. The Seneca Glass Company was the largest of the glass plants, occupying more than two and one-half acres. They produced glass tableware, including pitchers, tumblers, goblets, wine glasses, and soda tumblers—with a total output of 18,000 tumblers a day. The company prospered until 1896, at which time they moved to Morgantown, West Virginia, where they are still located.

MAMBOURG GLASS COMPANY (B).

This glass factory is another one of those that located here in 1887. They produced window glass in a new plant constructed for them south of town, west of the Hocking Valley Railroad (now Chessie System). In later years Bersted Mfg. Company occupied the building and Copeland Manufacturing Company is there now. The founder, Mr. Mambourg, was Belgian and imported workers from there. The factory continued operating until 1894.

56

BUTTLER GLASS COMPANY (C).

One reference source placed the location of this glass factory at the present site of the Fostoria Concrete Block plant on Sandusky Street, but another says it was across from the Sandusky Street school. The plant was named after William Buttler, who was one of the skilled glass-workers and credited with inventing some processes and machinery. They manufactured tableware. Production started in 1888 and continued until 1889, when the factory was destroyed by fire.

FOSTORIA NOVELTY GLASS COMPANY (C).

After Buttler Glass Company burned down, local businessmen reorganized and established a new factory. They produced glass tumblers in it until 1895, when the factory was again demolished by fire.

THE NICKEL PLATE GLASS COMPANY (D).

This glass factory was established here in 1888 by Wheeling, West Virginia, people. They manufactured blown goblets, milk glass, cranberry glass, and all kinds of tableware and lamps. The location was on the north side of McDougal Street, just west of the Nickel Plate Railroad. In 1891, this glass factory became part of the United States Glass Company. In 1895, the factory was destroyed by fire. Efforts were made to reorganize and rebuild but they were not successful.

FOSTORIA LAMP AND SHADE COMPANY (E).

As the company name indicates, they produced lamps and shades to replace the silk and textile shades which had been in common use. The factory location was south of the Nickel Plate Railroad, on the present site of Ohio Farmers Grain and Supply. The factory was completed in 1890. Pittsburgh interests as well as Fostorians were responsible for the organization and location of the plant here. At one time they were shipping 5,000 decorated lamps a day, 60% of all the lamps made in the United States. In 1894, the business was sold to Consolidated Lamp and Shade Company. In 1895, the factory burned and all of the management and skilled workers moved to Corapolis, Pennsylvania, to start another factory.

THE CALCINE GLASS COMPANY (F).

This was another window glass factory, organized in 1888, but did not start production until 1890. The location of the factory was east of the Hocking Valley Railroad, north of the Mambourg Glass Company. Production continued until 1894, when financial problems caused them to cease operations.

THE CROCKER GLASS COMPANY (J).

This was still another of the glass plants in Fostoria that produced window glass. The location was in the north end of town at the intersection of Poplar Street and Zeller Road. It was formed by Roswell H. Crocker, from one of the city's pioneer families. Historical data indicates it may have started production in 1890, and closed about the same time as the Calcine Glass Company in 1894.

Fostoria Incandescent Lamp Company and Fostoria Glass Specialty Company (G,B).

These two glass factories came into existence primarily through the efforts of J.P. Crouse and H.A. Tremaine, who in earlier years had started the carbon plant in Fostoria, which they later sold to National Carbon Company, Cleveland. Because of their business connections in Cleveland, these two astute businessmen saw the potential for manufacturing electric light bulbs and glass tubing. Fostoria Incandescent Lamp Company was started in 1897 and Fostoria Glass Specialty in 1899: one was on South Poplar Street at the east end of Fourth Street and the other was the building previously occupied by the Mambourg Company south of town. The Mambourg location was generally referred to as the "lower" plant and the other the "upper" plant. By 1910, both plants were successful enough to make them a prize purchase by General Electric Company, Cleveland. After the purchase by General Electric they expanded the operation to existing plants in Cleveland and other eastern Ohio locations. The "upper" plant discontinued operations in 1914; the "lower" plant in 1920.

Fostoria Glass Novelty Company (G).

When General Electric moved their glass-making operations elsewhere, local businessmen Earl Ash, Ralph Pillars, Mahlon Carr, and George Ridgeway organized Fostoria Glass Novelty Company and took over one of the "upper" buildings. The business didn't last very long, perhaps until 1916 or 1917.

Mosaic Glass Company (H).

Historical accounts indicate this glass factory was organized and financed by people connected with the Nickel Plate Glass Company who remained in Fostoria when it left town. It was located in a building on East North Street, which later was the location of the Fostoria Ice and Coal Company, and currently is occupied by Schreiner Construction Corp., 410 E. North Street. In 1892, they shipped 10 rail carloads of glass tile to the Columbian Exposition in Chicago. The life of this glass factory was short-lived, not more than a couple of years at most. A fire destroyed the plant in 1895. The company continued manufacturing in Fostoria until 1892, when they foresaw the day when free gas would no longer be available and their operating costs would increase substantially. They moved to Moundsville.

Pictured here is the Nickel Plate Glass Company on McDougal Street (D).

58

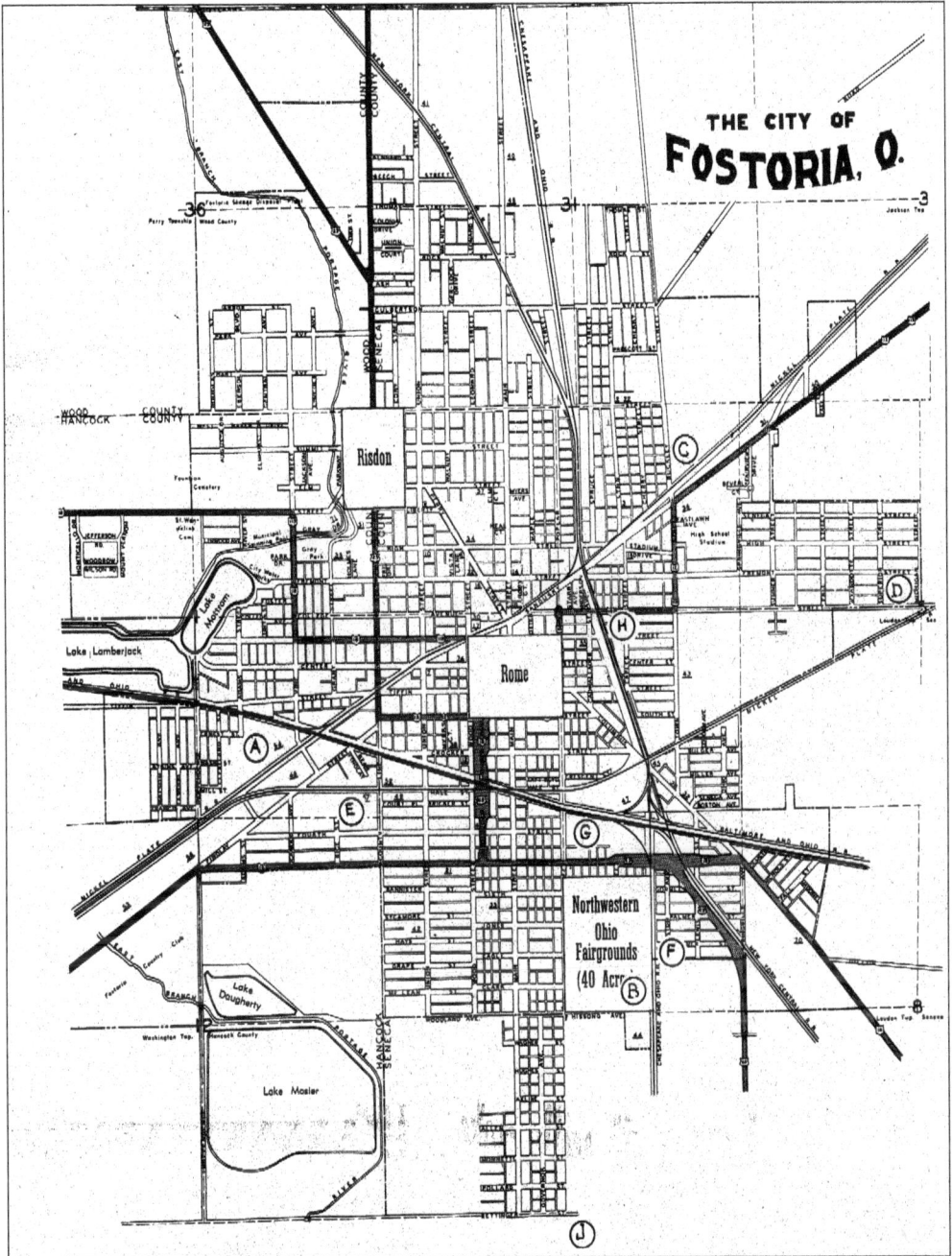

This map of Fostoria shows sites of glass companies marked with letters.

Pictured here is the Fostoria Incandescent Lamp Company on South Poplar (G).

Shown here is Fostoria Glass Specialty Company at the location of the Copeland Mfg. Company (B).

THE GLASS ERA
PEOPLE AND PRODUCTS

(August 23 and 31, 1978, and August 10 and 17, 1989)

Ray Coburn, a well-known citizen of Fostoria for many years and mayor, and respected by all those who know him, started in the glass industry at age nine at Macbeth Evans Company, Toledo, where his family then lived. The next year his family moved to Fostoria, and he went to work at General Electric's Upper Plant. Ray's father and brothers were also glassworkers. Like all young glassworkers he had to serve his apprenticeship until age 18 before being admitted to the union as a plate-mould blower. When he had attained that distinction, he went to a new GE plant at Niles, Ohio, and remained there five years. After that he worked in many other glass producing cities, winding up in Toronto, Canada, at which time he decided it was time to leave the industry. During his years as a glassworker he served for six years on the executive board of the American Flint Glass Workers Union, of which he is still a member.

Joe Eddy, in addition to being a glassworker, was also a sort of an inventor and tinkerer. He invented a washing machine, long before they were on the market, which provided agitation to clean the clothes and which also incorporated a gas heater underneath to heat the water. He never sold his patent or produced another machine.

Harry Edmonds was already a knowledgeable glassworker when he came to Fostoria to help establish the Fostoria Novelty Glass Company. When it failed, he became associated with the Anchor-Hocking glass factory in Lancaster, Ohio. At another period in his glass career, Edmonds was sent to China by General Electric for a year to teach the Chinese the art of glassmaking and to supervise a plant. When he returned to Fostoria to visit relatives and friends he brought me (Paul Krupp) a Chinese silk handkerchief. Silk was made by silk worms then. I was about ten or twelve at the time.

Frank O'Neil was a Fostorian who had a small machine shop here and was tinkering with ideas for the manufacture of machines for making certain glass items automatically and for bottle blowing. O'Neil saw some dishonest dealings in Fostoria, according to Carmen (Ash) Lyons, wife of Frank's nephew Richard, and decided to move his business to Toledo. After his move to Toledo in 1910, he perfected some of his ideas and manufactured machines that were used worldwide. In later years he sold his company to Owens-Illinois Glass Company, but retained his Montreal, Canada, plant, which was reputed to be the largest in the world for producing glassmaking machinery.

Michael J. Owens, like Frank O'Neil, was an inventor as well as a glassworker. Although he worked at a glass plant in Findlay, he was well known to Hugh Coburn, father of Ray Coburn. He later moved to Toledo to work for the Libbey Company and eventually produced a bottle-making machine, apparently about the same time O'Neil did. Edward Libbey, also a Toledoan, recognized the mechanical genius of Michael Owens and together, with Mike's mechanical know-how and Libbey's money, they revolutionized the making of glass, turning hand operations into the automatic machine age. The name Owens later became identified very importantly with the Owens-Illinois interests in Toledo. He is considered the "father" of the modern America Glass industry.

Carl Roland, deceased many years now, was another glassworker in Fostoria. He came from Denmark as a young man and boarded with my aunt and uncle, Mr. and Mrs. Frank Babcock. All of his earthly property was brought to the United States in a trunk from his homeland, and that trunk has been in the possession of this author for many years. After the glass factories in Fostoria closed, Roland did maintenance work at one or more of the retail businesses on Main Street. He was well know and liked, for many years was head usher at the Presbyterian Church, and he carried his Danish brogue from his landing in Fostoria until his death.

Henry Sturgess—I remember Mr. Sturgess, even though I was only a small child when he lived beside our family on Taft Boulevard. The family came to town when General Electric started making Iris glassware, to compete with Tiffany. Mr. Sturgess had worked for a number of glass factories in this country as well as in England, where he was born. He knew many well-guarded secrets of glassmaking and made a great contribution to the production of Iris glassware in the GE plant. His daughter, Mrs. Edith Babb, still resides in Fostoria.

An interesting aspect of the "Glass Days" was the large numbers of skilled workers who were brought to Fostoria from the European countries of Germany, France, Austria, and Belgium, where glassmaking was already established. Gordon Gray, in a paper prepared about the "Gas-Glass Days," tells how the foreign influx affected retail sales people: "The great majority of the foreign glassworkers who came here could not speak English. One of the immigrant's father, who was a clerk in a shoe store at that time, told me how his dad would study French at night in order to be able to wait on his foreign trade."

The glass factories, back in those early days, were notorious for hiring child labor, since there was no legislation prohibiting it. Gordon Gray, in his paper, reported all of the glass factories hired a percentage of boys between the ages of 10 and 16 as part of their work force. They were used to run errands for the skilled workers and to do odd jobs and otherwise assist the adult workers in any way possible. One of the glass companies built a special dormitory and imported a large number of orphans from the eastern seaboard to fill the labor need. One time, Ray Coburn was an official for the glass workers union and visited a local in the East. He was taken to the union hall and there found that most of the officers were boys still in short pants.

This photo shows one group of workers employed at the Upper Glass works, c. 1914–16.

Frosted "Victoria" Glass
Fostoria Glass Co.—1890

TOP ROW: Syrup pitcher; candy dish; fruit bowl; small dish; sugar bowl.
MIDDLE ROW: Rose bowl; punch cup; sauce dish; creamer; salt and pepper shakers; napkin ring; tumbler.
BOTTOM ROW: Celery holder; butter dish; spoon holder; pickle dish; cracker jar.

Examples of the famous Fostoria glassware are pictured here, from left to right, as follows: (bottom row) celery holder, butter dish, spoon holder, pickle dish, and cracker jar; (middle row) rose bowl, punch cup, sauce dish, creamer, salt and pepper shakers, napkin ring, and tumbler; (top row) syrup pitcher, candy dish, fruit bowl, small dish, and sugar bowl.

GREENHOUSES
(October 2, 1980)

(Editor's note: Don Etchen, one of many faithful readers of "Potluck," telephoned to suggest an article on the demise of greenhouses that once were in Fostoria. His interest stemmed partially from his employment at Enrights many years ago. Ralph Sackett and his son, Ralph Jr., known to Fostorians as "Sonny," contributed much of the data for this article.)

Fostoria's first greenhouse was established in 1880 by J.R. Black & Emerson Sackett. It was called "Fostoria Greenhouse" and was located near Fostoria's Academy. Then in 1905, E.R. Sackett went into business for himself on Maple Street, back of the family residence at 712 North Main Street.

Ironically, Sackett's dad didn't want him to go into the greenhouse business, but he went ahead with a contribution of $50 from his mother. If the business were still in operation today it would be 100 years old. Ralph Sackett, son of the founder, continued to operate the business until July 1969, when rising costs prompted him to close the business and dismantle the greenhouses, but maintain the office area for Sackett Gift Shop, now operated by Ralph Sackett, Jr., grandson of the founder.

Back one hundred years ago, when E.R. Sackett started on his own, he went door-to-door selling and taking orders. He wasn't afraid to work, and he must have learned the rudiments of business from his father, who had a farm on Buckley Road, and from his schooling at the rural Pankhurst one-room school and later in Fostoria City Schools. Sackett would work in his greenhouse all day, then go to the farm and cut wood at night to keep the growing business heated.

His business gradually expanded from three growing houses to thirteen, and he began to specialize in the growing of potted plants for all of the holidays. The business was soon one of the largest growers in northwestern Ohio, wholesaling flowers and potted plants to florists and flower shops in Toledo, Findlay, Bowling Green, Tiffin, Fremont, Kenton, Marion, Bucyrus, and smaller towns.

Ralph Sackett became a business partner in 1937 and managed the business until it closed in 1969. During his active management years he was elected to the board of directors of Ohio Florists Association, from 1955 to1957.

According to Ralph Sackett, few people realize the hard work, and long hours that go into the growing of flowers and plants up to the point of selling them. "Every type of plant we grew was different; each had to have a different type of soil, and each took a different temperature if the very best plant was to be produced, and to have it ready on time for the particular holiday. Fighting insects was always a problem. Some cut flowers had to be cut every day, including Sundays. Potted plants needed checking every day and watered often. We grew about five houses of poinsettias for the holidays and around 20,000 geraniums." Sackett recalled during World War II it was necessary to grow vegetable plants to qualify for the purchase of coal to heat the growing houses.

The other operators of greenhouses here included Enright's on South Union Street, later taken over by Claude and Clyde Payne, who came here from Missouri and took over after Tim Enright's death. Payne Brothers continued to grow plants and flowers until a year ago, when they too were forced to stop growing. Browning Payne, a son of one of the brothers, took over and has dismantled most of the growing houses, keeping only a small area and the office to assemble floral arrangements and sell cut flowers, produced by growers out of town.

The Stortz family had a small greenhouse across from Fountain Cemetery, catering to those who at the last minute would patronize them when arriving at the cemetery to decorate graves. Ray Hollenbaugh started a greenhouse on Columbus Avenue many years ago, which later was bought by Charles Zumpft, still later by Mike Besserman, and today is owned and operated by Jan & Paul's. It now grows only a small quantity of the flowers and bedding plants, the rest of their merchandise coming from the large growers elsewhere.

An aerial shot taken in 1954 shows the 13 growing houses that comprised E.R. Sackett's Fostoria Floral Company, later called Sackett's Greenhouse.

Here are two floats entered by Sackett's in a Memorial Day parade. The wheels of the buggy were covered with flowers from the Fostoria Floral Company. The second horse-drawn wagon was loaded with palms.

HENRY FORD DEALERSHIP
(July 20, 1978)

Ford Motor Company is celebrating its 75th anniversary this year. By 1959, they had produced 50 million cars. Earlier this year, they started seeking owners of the first model A cars produced in 1903. Only 1,078 cars of that model were built—82 are still in existence, many of them still in show quality condition.

At one time Ford seriously considered setting up a manufacturing plant in Fostoria, but it never materialized. You know the old story about the strong arguments the "big town" boys put up in favor of the cities, and the strong public relations programs they launch to beat out the smaller towns. Ford did own the spark plug plant in town in recent years. Willis J. Hakes started a Ford dealership here in 1908, just five years after Henry Ford started producing the famous 1903 model.

Ford had his ups and downs getting into the business of manufacturing cars—just like Hakes had his, getting into the car sales business. In fact, Ford started two times and failed before he was successful. The first time a group of wealthy investors formed a company and called it the Detroit Automobile Company. The company folded after a year and loss of $86,000. Ford had the mechanical talents, but his backers wanted to make a sophisticated car for the rich man. Ford wanted to build a low-priced vehicle for the masses.

In 1901, the Henry Ford Company was formed, but it lasted only three months before Ford pulled out. His idea of a car was one that could be made quickly and cheaply from contracted parts and didn't require a large manufacturing complex. Henry Ford had a friend, Alexander Malcomson, who put up the money, while he furnished the drawings, patents, and experience for the first prototype of the car he wanted to build. To assist them, Malcomson enlisted James Couzens, his bookkeeper, and Ford took on his friend and racecar engineering sidekick, Childe Harold Wills. In less than a year, Ford's plans for his new car were complete.

Hakes, like Henry Ford, was a farm boy. Born in 1885 on a farm south of Fostoria, he went to a one-room school, located at what is now south US 23 and Center Road. Hakes remembers, "My first job was working for Phil Peters, a neighboring farmer, doing threshing, haying, and general farming. Later I worked for the Cramer saw mill on the New Riegel Road. . . Judd Asire, the local undertaker, said to me, 'if I was as young as you are this is what I'd do' and he showed me the new Ford literature. So I went to Toledo to see about it and signed a contract to sell Fords, to accept one car every three months. It got so in 1920 we delivered 300 cars a year."

During World War I the Fordson tractor business took up the slack on car sales. Hakes recalled how one year he demonstrated and sold the tractors by plowing 1,100 acres for farmers.

The important dates for the Ford Motor Company local dealership follow:

1908—Willis J. Hakes established Ford dealership.
1910—Hakes rented room on east Tiffin Street, where Senior Citizens headquarters are today, sharing space with Reo agency the first two years.
1913–1920—Car sales soared.
1916—Hakes built second building on east South Street, opposite first one.
1949—Hakes revamped his first building and moved back into it and turned active management over to his son-in-law, Glen Marshall.
1967 (November)—Willis J. Hakes died, at which time his dealership for Ford cars was dissolved and Reineke Ford Inc. became the new dealer.

This photo shows the Willis J. Hakes dealership on East South Street c. 1910.

Here is a 1940 Ford assembly line.

ICE CUTTING
(August 5 and 12, 1982)

Do you remember when ice was used to refrigerate food in the home? Where did the ice come from and how was it preserved for use to keep food from spoiling? That's what today's story is about, which has taken two years of research.

One of the helpful items of research was when the *Review Times* published an Associated Press (AP) story about Charles Clark, who grew up in Old Greenwich, Connecticut, and still lives there, and who took part in harvesting ice when he was just a teenager, and is now a crusader for the subject. Why is Clark so serious about his effort? He says, "When we run out of oil . . . I do not say if we run out, but when . . . ice will be as necessary as it was before the days of the electric refrigerator."

Clark worked diligently to assemble a complete set of ice harvesting tools and they are lodged at the Stamford Museum and Nature Center, Stamford, Connecticut, where he often delivers lectures. One of the accompanying photos (page 69) shows the complete set of tools used in ice cutting: (1) marker for scoring the surface of the ice prior to cutting; (2) horse-drawn cutter (or plow) to cut through the ice except the bottom two inches; (3) pike poles for pulling or pushing the ice cakes; (4) grappling hook used to pull long rows of blocks into the ice house with block and tackle and horse; (5) ice caker and fork, used to break or split ice into separate blocks; (6) various sized tongs for handling separate blocks of ice when storing it in house and for removal; and (7) ice saw, used for hand cutting.

Here in Fostoria after the ice was cut, it was propelled through the open channel of water by the use of the pike poles by manpower to the icehouse, where the conveyor took over to carry them into the house. The storage houses were frame structures of double wall construction with 12 inches of sawdust used to insulate the walls.

The finished blocks, cut to size, were stored four tiers high. As the long blocks (still joined) traveled up the conveyor, workers used the ice caker and ice fork to break the long cake into finished size as they neared the door of the icehouse. When the house was filled with the first tier of ice blocks, the conveyor was moved so that the ice then entered the house through a door at a higher level and the operation was continued until all four levels were used and the house was filled. It was estimated that they cut and stored at least 60,000 pounds per hour.

Only the old-timers will remember how ice was utilized in the home to preserve food. The ice refrigerator was a wooden cabinet, approximately 4 1/2 feet high. The blocks of ice were put in a compartment on the top or side, and the ice chilled the interior air and it flowed downward through openings to keep the food placed on shelves cool. As the ice melted the water dripped through a tube to a pan placed under the refrigerator.

Consumers got their ice by horse-drawn delivery wagons, and later by trucks. I remember going to the icehouse with my little red wagon. Consumers had a card they would place in the window or door facing the street, indicating if they wanted ice. Ice was needed by consumers, merchants, restaurants, food packers and shippers, ice cream manufacturers, and others.

Luman says he believes 1913 was the last year ice was harvested from the reservoir in Fostoria. By that time the Fostoria Ice & Coal Company, headed by Harry Clore and Ralph Clink, had started to make ice in their plant on East North Street. Schreiner Construction Company now occupies that building. According to Kenneth Souder, one of the last employees of the Fostoria Ice and Coal, it closed in 1963. By then the electric refrigerator had totally replaced ice as a means of preserving food.

Ice cutting workers are pictured here at reservoir #1. Note the old water tower on the left.

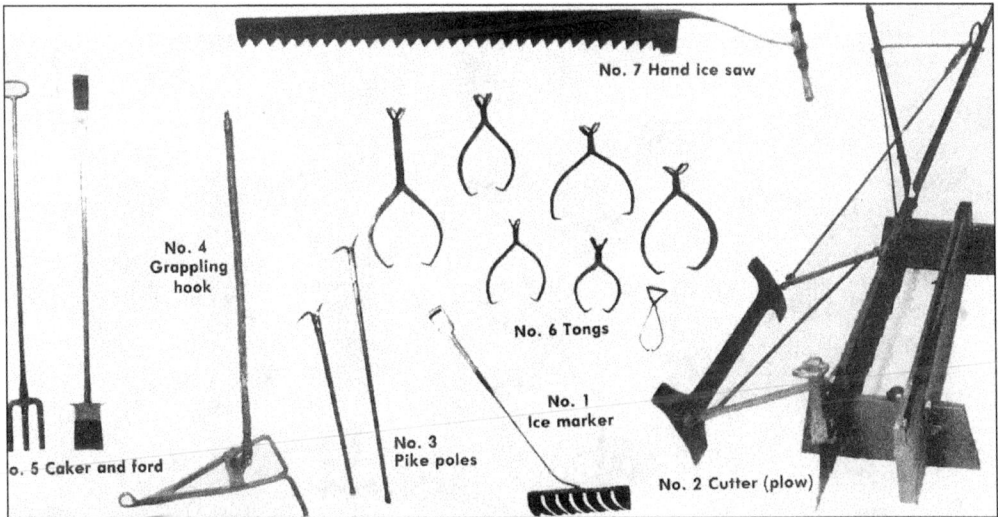

Pictured here is a complete set of tools used in ice cutting: (1) Ice marker; (2) cutter (plow); (93) pike poles; (4) grappling hook; (5) caker and ford; (6) tongs; and (7) hand ice saw.

JACKSON UNDERWEAR COMPANY
(January 24 and 31, and February 7, 1985)

The A.H. Jackson Company was a branch of the parent company in Fremont. For a few years the local factory was located in the old armory building (still standing) at McDougal and Poplar Streets. The need for larger factory space necessitated relocation. The September 28, 1912 issue of the *Fostoria Daily Review* revealed that Ron A.H. Jackson, of Fremont, was in Fostoria to close the deal for the site at the corner of East North and Potter Streets, and construction of the new building. J.D. McDonel was responsible for the sale of the land and J.H. Jones and N. Altweis for erection of the new factory. The land was purchased from the Commercial Bank & Savings Company for $3,000. According to Mr. Jackson, the new building would "provide modern facilities, not available in the old location, and provide space for fifty more sewing machines." Cost of the new 2-story structure was pegged to cost $10,000.

A.H. Jackson manufactured a line of ladies undergarments. In addition to the factory area on the second floor of the new building, the first floor has a retail store. Unlike most manufacturing establishments, A.H. Jackson Company provided a clean place for women to work. The work force was approximately 80, exclusive of management personnel. The only unfortunate working condition existed in the ever-present possibility of an employee running a needle in their fingers.

I have no knowledge of what prompted the A.H. Jackson Company to terminate manufacturing at their Fostoria factory. My recollection is that operations ceased in about 1924 or 1925. Although various commercial operations used the building for a number of years, it was in about 1941 that Gold Bond Furniture Company, owned by a Tiffin family, started a store at that site and continued until a couple of years ago.

Pictured here and the opposite page are employees at the Jackson Underwear Company, 1913.

The employees are listed as the following: Hattie Drenner, Amanda Krupp, Minnie Vandrier, Mrs. Dixon, Martha Dixon, Dora Vibrant, Oral Wright, Lena Weber, Iva Drake, Rose Kehn, Cora Martin, Adaline Ulman, Louise Atweis, Nora Walsh, Pauline Bick, Vera Caldwell, Irene Caldwell, Hilda Beck, Mary Snyder, Ethel French, Lulu Bemesderfer, Mary Duffield, Hattie Papenfus, Etta Wollensnydr, Gladys Duffy, Mr. Hamburg (manager), Maud Prebble, Ella Hallman, Glena Newhouse, Alvina Sussang, Lela Newhouse, Mary Doty, Elsie Buch, Eva Ulman, Emma Alwies, Florence Hamburg, Corduela Altweis, Ella Kehn, Ada Kieffer, Emma Vandrier, Dot Holderman, Anna Myers, Mary Hanna, Eulalia Altweis, Minnie Lorah, Lela Young, Grace Young, Goldie Pierce, Marion Cupps, Elizabeth Goshe, Mary Goshe, May Emmons, Emma Leesburg, ? Sheppard, Zeltha Stillwell, ? Adams, Martha Vibrant, ? Fausnaugh, and Mary Hubbard.

LUMBER MILLS
(April 19 and 26, and May 10, 1979)

These articles are about the lumber and woodworking factories, which sprang up in Fostoria in the last century and continued to exist for many years. The Koss, Parker, and German Lumber Company was formed by a group of Fostorians in 1894, when Fostoria was in its hey-day. It was located where the PK Company is now on West North Street, and occupied buildings on both sides of the street. Like most of the lumber companies of that day, they manufactured sash, blinds, doors, mouldings, and other wood products, for sale in the Fostoria area, but also shipped to eastern markets. At peak periods they employed 50 people. Eventually, the lumber company was sold to a large out-of-town company and was called Fostoria Lumber and Supply Company. The millwork building of the original company still stands on the triangle formed by North Street and the old LE&W railroad bed.

The Eureka Planning Mill and Lumber Company was started in 1887, and managed by John Portz, who resided at 123 North Countyline Street. The mill was located at the corner of East North and Cadwallader streets. The buildings are still standing, as part of the Gray Printing operation. As a boy I used to retrieve wood scraps from the mill to make various things I dreamed up. In the late 1920s or early 1930s the mill was purchased by the Lacost family—C. Tracey and Charles T. Lacost (Mrs. Joe Murrin's family), who

Here is an inside view of Stave and Barrel Company, later known as Seneca Lumber and Millwork.

owned three other mills and lumber yards in this area. The mill was renamed East North Street Lumber Company and was managed by Carl Oyler. After Oyler passed away, Joe Murrin became manager. It continued to operate until 1964, when Gray Printing purchased the property.

F.W. Fraver Saw and Planning Mill was located at the northeast corner of McDougal and Town Streets. Twelve men were employed year-round, and business was done throughout Seneca County. This mill was bought and consolidated with Seneca Lumber in 1919.

Cunningham, Portz, and Company was originally organized in 1869 by E.J. Cunningham, Nicholas Portz, and others, possibly including Charles Foster, since according to old records, Portz and Foster were associated in various business deals for more than 50 years. In 1882, the plant was rebuilt at 228 Findlay Street and became known as the Cunningham Manufacturing. At peak-capacity they employed 40 people making shipment to all parts of the country, but mainly eastern markets.

Others in the lumber and mill business in Fostoria many years ago included the following: B.F. Histe Hard and Soft Wood Lumber, 157 Elm Street; Campbell and Company Sash Factory, 143 W. North Street; Green and Heilman Planning Mill, established in 1873 by Martin V. Green and J.F. Heilman.

The Seneca Lumber and Millwork Inc. is 106 years old this year. It was and is another one of those Fostoria business enterprises that was started by local men, with local money, and grew and prospered by hard work and business acumen. Although the name has changed several times in those 106 years it has operated continuously, with some changes in the products made, but always related to wood. Originally, the company was known as the Fostoria Stave and Barrel Company, organized by Charles Foster, former Ohio Governor; John Noble, a cooper by trade; and E.J. Cunningham, also experienced in the wood industry.

The company manufactured their wood barrels from the tree, the entire process being done at the local plant. It was known as "the best equipped cooperage plant in northern Ohio, being fitted with all the best steam appliances," according to a descriptive booklet published about Fostoria's industry at that time. The logs came from the local forests that surrounded Fostoria back then. Barrels for flour, glass, carbon, and other products were manufactured.

All of the flour barrels for the Harter Milling Company (predecessor to Mennel Milling Company) and for other Fostoria companies were manufactured in the local plant, and shipments were made to many customers in the eastern part of the United States. In 1919, the original company bought and consolidated the F.W. Fraver Mill and changed the name to the Fostoria Building and Supply Company, since the company's business had gravitated from the earlier products of barrels and staves to the manufacture and sale of building materials. In 1921, the company name was again changed to the Seneca Lumber and Millwork Company, at which time the Seneca Wire and Manufacturing Company assumed control. Under the leadership of L.E. Kinn, president, the company grew; by 1938 the annual payroll had reached $100,000. The company was then operating a retail lumberyard, selling paint, lumber, building materials, and manufacturing woodwork for public buildings such as schools, colleges, hospitals, government buildings, hotels, office buildings, and homes.

During the World War II years, Seneca Lumber was deeply involved in government work, furnishing millwork for government housing, and making a variety of items, such as foot lockers, ammunition boxes, tote boxes, and all kinds of cabinets. At one time during their peak business years, Seneca had offices in New York, Pittsburgh, Cleveland, and Detroit. In 1954, the company was acquired by a Toledo company, and became known as Seneca Lumber and Millwork Company Division Hixon-Peterson Lumber Company. In 1959, 11 Fostorians purchased the plant and operation, incorporating it under the name of Seneca Lumber and Millwork, Inc.

Some of the company's specialty millwork includes work at Cedar Point, the conference table in the Cabinet Room at the Ohio State Governor's office, and oak doors for the library for Sisters of St. Francis, Sylvania, Ohio.

MANN FUNERAL
(October 11 and December, 9, 16, and 23, 1982)

It began as Mann Brothers Undertakers around 1910. There was no such business as a "funeral home." Funerals were conducted either in the home or at a church. The undertaker prepared the body and made other burial arrangements. They located at 115 West Center Street in the Burtscher Building.

In 1916, after the death of Nicholas Burtscher, his home at 217 West Center Street was purchased by the Mann brothers, Asa and Jay, for their funeral home. When the Mann brothers moved their business to the Burtscher property, they and their father, Charles, a woodworker, started making wooden caskets. The manufacturing facilities were in a building in the rear of the funeral home. Their caskets were shipped to funeral directors in a number of states.

Another accomplishment of the father, Charles, was a motor-driven hearse, replacing their old horse-drawn vehicle. He built a hearse cab on an Allen car chassis. After Asa and Jay died, the business was taken over by sons John and Richard.

The home remained at the Center Street location until 1959 when they moved to the former George M. Gray home on North Countyline Street. In 1980 the home became known as Mann-Hare Funeral Home when Richard Mann retired and Thomas Hare became the principal operator, with John still associated.

Pictured here is the Mann Brothers Funeral Home at 217 West Center Street.

Here is the Mann Brothers horse-drawn ambulance, *c.* 1910, with Asa (left) and Jay (right) Mann.

Shown here is a Mann funeral procession in 1911, consisting of 13 horse-drawn carriages, at the corner of Wood and West Center Streets.

OHIO SAVINGS AND LOAN
(May 14, 1981)

It was on September 18, 1915, that the Articles of Incorporation were filed with the Secretary of State of Ohio by Walter Witherspoon, who became the association's attorney. On November 10, 1915, 30 local shareholders met with Witherspoon, acting as temporary secretary, and Carl Smith, local insurance agent, as temporary chair-person. At that meeting, the first Board of Directors was unanimously elected as follows: L.J. Eshelman, druggist; W.J. Wagner, men's clothing; A.C. Hoyt, seeds; W.G. Emergy, dentist; Frank Kiebel, dry goods; Frank Gebert, dentist; M.M. Carr, furniture and industrialist; A.J. Vogel, tailor; and James Cullen. At that meeting, Cullen was elected the first president; Carl Smith, secretary; and Witherspoon, attorney. Carl Smith's insurance office at Room 3 in the Andes Block became the first office for the new saving and loan company.

In May 1917, it moved to 117 West Center Street in the Burtscher Building, where Fostoria Appliance Outlet is now. In February 1927, the Association moved to the corner of Tiffin and Main Streets, where they remained for 10 years. In 1937, the company moved into the First National Bank building at the corner of Main and Center Streets, which had been vacated by that bank when it took over the Union National Bank building, where Tri-County is now. In December 1940, J.F. Peter, a well-known Fostoria businessman, was elected president. Shortly thereafter, J.J. Seever was employed as an assistant bookkeeper to Edyth Allen, who had continuous employment for 41 years with the Association. With the death of Fred Gerlinger in 1942, Seever ("Jakie," as he was known to most everyone) was named secretary and managing officer and held that office until his death in 1965.

In 1948, it became known that the First National Bank building was to be demolished to make way for a new 1-story structure, which eventually S.S. Kresge occupied. Announcement of the demolition was received with remorse by many Fostorians, since it was a landmark, having been built by the Emerine family in the late 1800s. It shows up in many postcards and photos taken during that period. Professional people occupying offices on the upper floors had to find new quarters, including the Ohio Savings. By then the association figured it was time to purchase their own location. It selected the building on the southwest corner of North and Main Streets, which was the A. Beesch Tea Company on the ground floor. So in 1948, the association moved to this its fifth location.

From 1948 until 1965, the Association had spectacular growth, and it became evident that the Main and North location was not adequate for the future. In 1968, one of Fostoria's prime locations, the large impressive Dan McCarthy property at 133 West Tiffin Street, just west of the Municipal Building, became available for purchase. The association purchased that property, and after demolishing the home, built its new headquarters there in October of 1969. In 1974, OS&L opened a branch office in the Fostoria Plaza.

The growth of the association during the past 66 years is shown by the following figures: capital stock subscribed in 1915 was $50,000, but paid up subscription at the end of the first year were only $8,350. Loans during the early days usually amounted to less than $1,000. At the end of 1980, first mortgage loans were $54,504,910 with total assets of $63,346,021.

The current directors of the association are L. Glen Marshall, chairperson of the board; Thomas L. Monasmith, president; Loren Chalfin, chairperson; James G. Gray, Thomas L. Krupp, Richard Norton, William O'Donnell Sr., Ralph Sackett Jr., and Melvin Schreiner. Directors emeritus are R.L. Collins, Ralph Sackett Sr., and Dwight Hazeltine. Present employees are Marjorie Thomas, Luann Fleming, Becky Cramer, Jane Burns, Jami Cassidy, Janie Fairley, Lisa Adams, Terri Williams, Norma Martinez, Jan Schlesselman, Becky Reinhart, Becky Heiser, Joanne Pierce, Jennie Mortimer, Linda Wangler, and Barbara Fox.

In 1948, the Association moved to its fifth location at the corner of North and Main Streets, with the time and temperature sign, which readers will remember.

TELEPHONE COMPANY
(February 17 and 24, 1983)

Six years after Alexander Graham Bell invented the telephone in 1876, Fostoria was introduced to the amazing new way to talk to the butcher, grocer, baker, doctor, and friends—anywhere in town—without leaving their homes. It was in the March 17, 1882 edition of the *Fostoria Review* that a news item announced that petitions were being circulated to obtain a sufficient number of signatures to guarantee a local phone exchange. A month later it was reported that a franchise had been granted to the Midland Telephone Company to provide the new service in Fostoria. Shortly thereafter, on June 6, 1882, it was available. Initially 25 businesses and three residences signed up.

The telephone exchange office of this new business was on the second floor in a building at the corner of Main and North, where the Botto Block was later built. The 1889–90 city directory showed a listing for the Central Telephone Station, with George Sheibley as manager. When Midland started telephone service here, the venture was financed by selling toll coupon books valued at $5 and $10. At the end of 1883, the number of telephone customers on Midland's lines was 56, up from the initial figure of 28. In that same year, long distance calls could be made from Fostoria to Toledo, Findlay, Tiffin, and Fremont.

In 1889, another telephone exchange, Citizens Telephone and Message Company, introduced telephone service in Fostoria. J.C. Rhodes was manager. It was located at 116 1/2 North Main Street and later on up to the time of its dissolution in 1915, it was at 121 East Tiffin Street. During those competitive years of the two exchanges, most businesses and professional offices had both phones.

March 21, 1895, was a gala day for Fostoria, especially those who had Central Union telephones. It marked the opening of long distance lines from Fostoria to Cleveland, New York, Buffalo, Pittsburgh, Chicago, and Indianapolis. Accounts tell how hundreds of people came to the reception at the Earl Hotel, East Tiffin Street, where Central Telephone arranged 40 telephones around a table so folks could listen in on conversation and music in distant cities. In 1922, Central Union became part of Ohio Bell.

I recall the first telephone call I ever made. It was placed from Amanda Sayre's millinery store on the second floor of the building at Main and Center, where City Loan is now. The call was to Wilbur Sheely, a friend who had moved from McDougal Street to a farm where Meadowlark Park is now. Their house still stands at that location. Back then, to place a call you lifted the receiver and a telephone operator said "Number Please." Wilbur's number was 985. I remember it after at least 65 years. I gave the operator the number and soon was talking with Wilbur. I don't recall our conversation, but it was thrilling to place the call on the device. The accompanying photo shows the typical telephone equipment back then, including the "hello girls" seated at the switchboard, where the "caller" was joined with the "called" by the operator.

Many readers will recall when the Ohio Bell office and exchange were in the building on East North Street. Customers paid their bills there and operators and installation and repair employees were headquartered there, too. In later years, Ohio Bell built a new building just east of 117 East North Street and installed all of the equipment for the new local dial system which went into effect in 1940. The new building also housed the business offices. With the new dial system, the only need for operators was for certain long distance phone calls and other operator-assisted calls. For those types of calls, the reduced staff of operators was located in the Findlay Bell office.

"Hello girls" are at work on the second floor of the Ohio Bell building at 117 East North Street, where the operators completed calls. Vera (Earl) Stoneberger is seated at desk in rear. Dorothy Flechtner is standing in foreground, left. Bonnie Welker, chief operator at the time is standing in the center at rear. Virginia (Hicks) Krupp and Jestene Welker are sitting on high stools at left. The nine operators at the switchboards could not be identified.

This 1931 photo shows Bell employees, from left to right, as follows: (front row) Beryl Lanker, commercial department cashier; Helen Wolfelt, operator; Lauretta Hutchins, assistant commercial cashier; Margaret "Peg" Massie, operator; Florence Boyer, supervisor; Jestene Welker, chief operator, and Ruth Roberts of Findlay; (back row) Helen Polta, chief operator; James Dawson, lineman and phone installer; Howard Youngston, lineman; Lawrence Zimmerman, plant chief; Theron Greenlee, test board chief; Mabel Bennett, operator; Clarence Mellen, commercial manager; Vera Earl, chief operator; and Nellie Yates, operator.

WOOLWORTH
(June 28, 1979)

One hundred years ago a man by the name of Frank Winfield Woolworth started a store in Utica, New York, and called it the "Great Five Cent Store." That was the beginning of what eventually became the F.W. Woolworth chain of stores that spread around the world and became more commonly known as the "Five and Ten Cent Store." Nothing sold for more than 10¢. Further significance of the 100th anniversary for some Fostorians is the fact that Dean C. Eger, who grew up here and became associated with Woolworth when a young man, made this his lifetime connection, and finally became executive buyer in their New York office, retiring in 1962 (see page 108).

Frank Winfield Woolworth had an exceedingly difficult time in his early life, a circumstance which probably contributed to his persistence and will to succeed. His first employers even thought he was not intelligent enough to wait on customers and he wound up washing windows, delivering, sweeping, and doing other menial jobs. He even worked for a time without pay, just to get experience. Later he worked 15 hours a day for 50¢—not 50¢ per hour, but 50¢ per day. Imagine that!

His early work experience brought on a nervous breakdown and he went home to his parents, near Watertown, New York, to be nursed back to health by his loving mother, who convinced him he would succeed and become rich some day. When he was well again he borrowed $300 and opened a store of his own, in Watertown. Very simply, he laid his merchandise out on tables, pricing it at not more than 10¢—much of it for 5¢. His first three stores failed, but on his fourth try he found the secret for merchandising, and he made $2.50 the first week. He opened 12 more stores that year and continued to grow into the nationwide chain—the first of its kind—and eventually worldwide. The two secrets that spelled success for Woolworth were the importance of a good location, and the need for a variety of merchandise.

When F.W. Woolworth Company decided to open a store in Fostoria it was 1916. The first manager was Ray V. Nicholson. Our town was booming. On Saturdays, especially in the evening, it was difficult to get through the crowds that thronged the streets and stores. That might seem an exaggeration, but it is a fact. Everybody came "uptown" on Saturday night. Woolworth had a good location in Fostoria. It was the Botto Block, one of the town's newer buildings, at North and Main.

Older Fostorians will remember the variety of merchandise that was displayed on the counters in the local store—for not more than 10¢. There was a large candy counter, also ribbon, yarn, greeting cards, drugs, notions, hardware, muslin, stationery, woodenware, jewelry, records, paint, and much more. The music department in some of the larger Woolworth stores, where sheet music was sold, was popular because they had a piano and pianist, where songs of that era, such as "I Cried for You," "Toot Toot Tootsie," and "Five Foot Two, Eyes of Blue" could be played for the customers to stimulate sales.

Those who especially remember the local store and merchandise are those former employees still living. Some still reside here. One of those is Dorothy (Kuhn) Vanderhoff, who worked there starting in the 1920s and who helped assemble the following list: Shirely Good, Erline Reidling, Joan Haughawart, Betty Zeigler, Jim Harris, Ann Weiker, Barbara Conrad, Donna Musser, Sarah Martin, Neva Bomer, Cheri Lou Jackson, Pat Williams, Patty Russell, Janet Gillespie, Bonnie Mogart, Roger Ferguson, Jim McCarley, Doris Clark, Audrey Watkins, Nellie Moyer, Vera Hoover, Maxine Wilcox, Richard Wilcox, Hattie Eckert, Leah Elkert, Lavonne Henline, Ruth Henline, Betty Davison, Vernie Stearns, Maragret Bentz, Thelma Racey, Mrs. Fouts, Margaret Koons, Geneview Schaull, Doris Roberts, Madelin Rinehart, Pearl Herbert, Flossie Rigby, Beatrice Thrailkill, Maxine Warner, Helen (Fruth) Spooner, Helen (Leeseburt) Cotter, Etta May (Kindmon) Wagner, Grace Framkfarther, William "Skeet" Boyd, and Mary Arnoldi.

Pictured here is the Woolworth store on the first floor of the southeast corner of Main and North Streets.

Here is an interior view of Fostoria's Woolworth store and employees, c. 1926. They are, from left to right, Genevier Schaul (Yates), Margaret Kotterman (Fox), Hazel Hindmon, Leola Henry (Crunkilton), Betram "Burkie" Kane, O.T. Shank (manager), Francis Marley (local attorney), Clara Omlor (Sutliff), Helen Fruth (Spooner), Edith Frankenfield (Swinehart), Bea Thraikill (Woostenburg), and Mary Shelt.

STONEWORKER
BRADFIELD HAMILTON

(September 5, 1985)

(This article was done with help from Chet Kieffer, Ray Coburn, Mrs. Robert Corwin, a niece of the Hamiltons, and Mrs. Dorothy (Hampshiere) Merrit, a great-niece of the Hamiltons.)

Thousands of people living in Fostoria and the surrounding area have visited Fountain Cemetery, many of them hundreds of times. By doing so, they have passed under the stone archway at its main entrance on Van Buren Street. Master craftsman Bradfield Hamilton was responsible for this archway, and the rest of the stone entrance, including the stone boat in the center of the enclosure, where flowers are planted each spring. The cemetery arch and fence were constructed by Hamilton in 1917, when Frank Kelly was service director and S.D. Newman was cemetery superintendent.

He also constructed a stone fence at his residence at the corner of North Union and Ash Streets and several small mausoleums at Fostoria Cemetery, including one for his own family. Both Mrs. Merritt and Mrs. Corwin told me that the stones used to construct the cemetery masterpieces and the fence around his home on North Union Street were a variety of small meteorites shipped here from New Jersey.

Bradfield Hamilton was married to Della Jones, one of five daughters of Mr. and Mrs. John Jones, well-known in Fostoria at that time.

The familiar arch, fence, and boat at the entrance of Fountain Cemetery, was designed and constructed by Bradfield Hamilton.

Four

OUR RECREATION

BICYCLING
(August 10, 1978)

Wilbur Wright and his brother Orville ran a bicycle shop in Dayton, Ohio, before they made and flew their airplane. They made fine custom cycles for those who could afford them. Glen Olds, who made the Oldsmobile, was in the bike business first, as was Glenn Curtiss of aviation fame.

Bicycles, back 50 to 100 years ago, were a far cry from the 10-speeds of today. Then, they were quite simple and fairly easy to maintain. Some of the early ones even had solid tires (not inflatable) so punctures were not a problem—and early ones didn't even have chains to break because propulsion was by pedaling directly to the large front wheel.

When I was a boy, I remember that bicycles were used by many adults for transportation and for carrying on their work. There was Whitney Abbott, who lived on Maple Street and worked at the Mennel Mill and used a bicycle to go to and from work. There was C.A. Ward, the musician who pedaled his bicycle all over town, going to the homes of his pupils to teach them. Of course all of us newspaper carrier boys had bicycles as they do today.

Like other Fostorians, I remember Father Weber of St. Wendelin, who used a bicycle to carry him about town on business and for calling on his parishioners. His trusty vehicle didn't use a chain drive—it used a gear driven drive shaft. And there was Weaver the photographer; Copley the bicycle dealer; DiCesare the city lamp lighter; Otto Huth and Otto Hettle, both printers, who rode bikes to work; and scores of other Fostorians who valued the bike as a means of sure, safe, economical transportation. Many high school students back in my era (1920–1923), who lived on the periphery of Fostoria, or even several miles in the country, pedaled their way to get their education.

Looking at an old photo of the Andes building, I discovered that the Fostoria Bicycle Club had their headquarters there—their name was mounted between the second and third floor windows. The Fostoria Bicycle Club was made up of men only. Albums owned by Fostorians Ray Dell and Mr. and Mrs. Lawrence Droll are full of pictures taken as they rode around the countryside. Some of the pictures indicate that they may have traveled as far as Tiffin.

About the same period of time as the existence of the Fostoria Bicycle Club (the 1880s) there also existed another group in town known as the Harrison and Morton Bicycle Club. They advertised themselves as "the only political organization on wheels in the U.S." They campaigned for President Harrison and Vice President V.P. Morton in 1884. The accompanying photo shows what an outstanding appearance they must have made in their snazzy outfits, with helmets on their high-wheel bikes, as they pedaled about town.

When I was a boy there were bicycle races for the youth—not drag racing cars. Frank Copley, the leading bicycle dealer then, was the principal figure in staging the races and soliciting the prizes from local business men for the awards. The races were held on suitable streets or highways—one of them being the Findlay Road starting at the intersection of West Independence and going west toward Arcadia. There was high excitement among the participating youth in the races. Some of the racers had racing bikes (not variable speed) with larger rear sprockets for higher speed, but many participated with their ordinary bikes, depending on their leg strength for speed.

F.A. "Frank" Copley had his shop at 132 East Center Street for many years. My first "used" bike came from his place. In later years he moved to 105 Perry Street. Then there was Bill Leatherman, who sold and repaired bicycles at his shop at 609 Columbus Avenue. L.O. Sprout's Bicycle and Fix-it Shop was in a basement location under the First National Bank on East Center Street, but later moved to 146 West Center Street.

Pictured here are members of Harrison & Morton Bicycle Club, from left to right, as follows: (front row) Charles Backenstos, unknown, unknown, Frank Hale, and Will Connor; (middle row) unknown, unknown, Andy Mergenthaler, Clair Van Blarcum, unknown, and George Enos; (back row) George Cunningham, unknown, unknown, George Johnson, Charlie Brown, Dave Balmer, and Harry Mickey, (last three unknown).

Here is a Fostoria club member with his hi-wheeler.

CIRCUS
(June 1, 1978)

"The circus is coming to town!" That was the exclamation on the lips of Fostorians—both young and old, many years ago. It was a big event—an all-day event—and they were BIG circuses that hit our town, back then. The billboards, telephone poles, and business windows were plastered with signs weeks in advance, announcing the dates for the extravaganza.

At the crack of dawn on the big date, circus lovers would be on hand at the railroad yards to see them unload. Railroad yard? Yes, the circus with all its paraphernalia, animals, and people came by train—their own cars, too, all except the railroad's engine that pulled them. There were many flat-cars for animal cages, specially built cars for the elephants, sleeping cards for the performers. All cars were decorated and labeled with the circus' name and colors. It was a great spectacle to see, and a cheer went up when the train was sighted coming down the track.

Watching the circus unload was just the start of the full-day's event. The fans then made their way to the field where the circus was held to watch the big tent go up, to see the elephants move the wagons and cages into position. Dads watched too until it was time to go to work. The rest of the family stayed on until set-up operations were completed, munching on snacks, looking at all the animal cages, reading the sideshow banners proclaiming the world's smallest human, the fat woman, the dancing girls—and lots more. All this was free, but it got the onlookers steamed-up to return for the afternoon and evening performances.

Then there was the noon-time parade down Main Street. The parade route would be packed with spectators to hear the steam calliope and band, to see the brilliantly decorated cages with the wild animals pulled by teams of six or eight horses, pretty girls riding on elephants, clowns with big, wobbly feet, red noses and bald heads—and so much more.

Young and old alike know the name Ringling Brothers—it's the only big circus left from the old days. Back when I was a boy there was Barnum and Bailey, Ringling Brothers, and Hagenbeck and Wallace. They all showed up in Fostoria, because of the railroad facilities here. They could arrive and leave Fostoria from all directions. Fox Field, on West Lytle at Independence Road, was one of the spots where circuses set up years ago. A farm field farther west on Findlay Road was also used, as well as the show grounds on South Main Street.

One year I carried water for the elephants and helped set-up the bleachers in the big tent, to earn a pass for the show. Another time I worked in the mess tent where the circus laborers ate. I'll never forget how they devoured the large bowls of boiled potatoes and fish, bread and coffee, that us kids carried from the cook tent. All for a pass to see the big three-ring show.

Musicians in circus bands, at least in the old days, were excellent, as Dr. J.N. Kiebel would verify if he were living today. "Nick" never passed up an opportunity to play his clarinet in a circus band.

(Editor's note: The photos accompanying "Potluck" today were taken many years ago when Ringling Brothers and Barnum and Bailey combined show made its last appearance at Fox Field in Fostoria. Photos taken by my son, Nathan Krupp.)

Elephants file off the railroad cars as Fostorians watch.

The "Big Top" goes up with a little help from pachyderms.

COLLECTING GLASS ITEMS
(February 25, 1988)

All the history of the past isn't contained in history books. Some readers may say, "How can that be?" Today's article will answer the question! There are many family histories which never get into public print. Many family histories are hand-written or typed and copied, and circulated within the family. There are antique cars, toys, horse-drawn buggies, furniture, books, and much more that only come to public attention in museums or perhaps when they are placed on sale.

Another category of history is made up of the variety of bottles, jars, wine sets, decanters, pill cans, ink stands, insulators, flasks, lightning rods, target balls, fire extinguishers, and many other items—all made of glass—which today are matters of history. Thousands upon thousands of those historical items have found their way to "dumping-areas" all over America, including Fostoria. Many of those areas have been covered over more than once, and "diggers" may dig 3 or 4 feet to find the valuable relics of the past.

The hobby of collecting glass items has intrigued those who are interested in history, especially bottles used for medicine, milk, and drinks. Every year, according to the "Whittle Marks," published by the Findlay Antique Bottle Club, hundreds of previously unknown bottles and jars are discovered.

Finding unknown milk bottles, for example, is proof of a dairy long forgotten. Medicine and drug bottles are glass items used extensively many years ago. Here in Fostoria there were many drug stores that filled prescriptions in glass which contained the druggists name molded into the bottle. Also, some doctors used bottles with their name molded into the glass. Some well-known medicine manufacturers put their products in glass that contained their name and product name molded into the glass.

Fostoria had doctors practicing here many years ago, and some of them had their own bottles. What a thrill for "diggers" to turn up one or more of them, indentifying a local doctor. Doctors the author recalls are Hale, Henry, Rosendale, Miller, Teycraft, Norris, Hatfield, Palmer, and Leonard.

Some people collect bottles for decoration. Because of the variety of color, shape, and size, bottles can flatter most any area. Medicine and druggist bottles add an interesting and unusual look to the bathroom. Perfume on the dresser and flasks in the den or living room add class and character to any decor. Canning jars make excellent air-tight, moisture-proof canister sets. And a colorful bottle will transform any sunny window into an extraordinary showplace. Still others collect bottles for the investment potential. Rare old bottles, like other fine quality antiques, seldom go down in value. Some collections have been sold at a substantial profit. Finding a glass item may be worth $10, $20, $30, or much more.

Findlay Antique Bottle Club, founded in 1976 with only five members, has grown to include 23 families from all over northwestern Ohio. Membership is open to anyone with an interest in old bottles, jars, insulators, or related items. In addition to the regular monthly meeting, the club stages an annual show, sale, and picnic each summer. At that time, they have a swap session, games for the kids, bingo, and bottle drawing. They have also had "club digs," which have proved to be lots of fun. At their well-attended Christmas party, many nice bottles are always included in the gift exchange.

The various glass items shown in this photo are the property of Fostorian Rodger Bartley, a member of the Findlay Antique Bottle Club. The items are just a few of the large collection he has "dug" in the relatively short time he has been involved in the hobby. Item identifications are as follows: (1) Aunt Jemima bank; (2)Union Fruit jar; (3) Ohio Pottery jug; (4) Paige Dairy, Toledo, milk bottle; (5) Frank Miller crown dressing container; (6) Davis container for pain killer; (7) Blue soda bottle, City Bottling Works, Toledo; (8) Blue glass soda bottle, Jacob Voekler & Company, Cleveland; (9) Amber Coca Cola bottle, Dayton; (10) Clear soda bottle, Wagner Bros., Tiffin; (11) Soda Bottle, Fostoria Bottling Works, Fostoria; (12) Soda bottle, Star Bottling Works, Toledo; (13) Clear soda bottle, Wagner Bros., Tiffin; (14 and 15) Cobalt blue medicine bottles; (16) Eshelman & Harbaugh Company, Fostoria, Bromo Seltzer bottle; (17) Bromo Seltzer bottle; (18) John Weith & Bros.; (19) Noxzema bottle.

FAIR
(May 8. 1980)

Few Fostorians are aware Fostoria had a 40-acre fair ground back in the 1880s. Its location is shown on the accompanying map (page 91). The Northwestern Ohio Fair Company was privately owned by 166 stockholders and governed by officers and board of directors.

The first fair was during the week of September 19, 1886, and as is often the case with fair-week, there were intermittent downpours of rain the opening day, mixed with some sunshine, according to news stories. However, Wednesday's crowd was estimated at 2,000, Thursday 4,000, Friday 8,000 to 10,000, and Saturday 5,000.

Back then, Seneca County didn't have a fair, and Fostoria's was said to be as fine as any in Ohio, with modern buildings, a fine grandstand, and a half-mile track 60 feet wide. It was considered by all the harness horse drivers to be the best in Ohio.

The fair boasted an Art Hall, Carriage Hall, Main Hall, ample stalls for exhibiting horses, cattle, sheep, swine, poultry, and work-oxens. Like today's fairs there were exhibits of fruit, vegetables, paintings, and handiwork. Practically every commercial enterprise in Fostoria had an exhibit booth. Bands from Bloomdale, Pemberville, Republic, and the Emerald Band of New York City furnished music during the fair.

One of the masterpieces in Art Hall was a large photograph of a little daughter of O.Z. Werner, taken by the instantaneous process, just as the little child laughingly made a remark. The picture was admired by hundreds of attendants, and took first prize. It was taken by Charles Gribble, who had a photographic studio here then.

The first year's fair was said to be successful and profitable. The Northwestern Ohio Fair Company continued to own the fair and to present a program for perhaps five or six years. We don't know why it was discontinued. It was a great event for Fostoria while it lasted. It seems like our town was always "out in front." There must have been an extremely enthusiastic and able group of civic leaders who led our town.

A horse race is captured here in progress at Fostoria's fairgrounds.

Here is a map showing the location of the fairgrounds in southeast part of town.

GOLF
(November 21, 1984)

This article and the accompanying photo are about one group of boys who caddied at the Fostoria Country Club during its early days. Today, golfers use motorized carts to carry their bag of clubs and to ride around the golf course. Back then, golfers employed boys to carry their bag of clubs and to chase balls. Being on a golf course, the caddies learned much about the game, such as the use of the various clubs and when to use each, and many other pointers best learned from good golfers. Most of the boys shown in the accompanying photo became golf enthusiasts in later years, some of them excellent players who continued to play at the club where they once caddied.

The story is told that one day, at the end of a round of golf when the sun was setting, and a golfer named Christy was at the end of the course, John Lee ran ahead to retrieve the ball in the event it was lost. Christy walloped the ball and then yelled "fore." Lee turned around to look and—wham—the ball hit him squarely on the forehead, knocking him out cold. Christy ran to John, picking him up and carrying him to his car. When he regained consciousness Christy took him to Dr. Henry at John's request. Leaving him there, Christy put a $20 bill in John's hand and said, "If that isn't enough, I'll make it right." Dr. Henry cleaned and bandaged the laceration and then, according to John, asked him how much money he had to give for the treatment. John explained about the $20 and the doctor reportedly said, "You'll make a profit on this treatment." Dr. Henry was the grandfather of Josephine, John Lee's present wife.

Robert Wagner, a well-known Fostorian of that era, was an avid golfer and also caddie-master there. Other golfers who frequented the local course included: Clarence Brown, president, American Railway Signal; Walter Witherspoon, attorney; Dr. M.E. Seiple, dentist; Dr. M.A. Prudden, osteopath; W.O. Hays, insurance agent; Glenn H. Eaton, druggist; E.R. Pillars, industrialist; and Earl Ash, farmer/banker.

Country Club Caddies of years ago pictured here, from left to right, are Al Knox, John Lee, Leland Gorrill, Maurice Schart, Frank Hemersbach, Orlo Luhring, Ray Krupp, Walter Fruth, Truman Weimerskirch, Phil Degan, "Mope" Bill Doyle, and Harold Krupp.

HORSESHOES
(December 8, 1988)

What happened to that once popular sport of pitching horseshoes? Many years ago, when this author was a lad, there were many teams, some consisting of men and some of boys. The men pitched with shoes used on full grown horses, and the younger set often used the smaller, lighter-weight shoes used on ponies.

Many readers will recall the "clang" of the shoes as they hit the stakes at which they were aimed and often found their mark as a "ringer." It was a great game of fun and skill that often was played in the evenings until it became too dark, unless there was artificial light to permit the game to continue. Horseshoe pitching was usually a pastime often included at family reunions and other outdoor gatherings.

In 1934, the Fostoria Horseshoe Club finished the season with an undefeated slate and a string of 21 consecutive victories. In the last game of the season they easily defeated Clyde 799 to 389, to gain undisputed possession of the championship of the Northern Ohio Horseshoe League. Fostoria tossed 351 single ringers and 32 doubles.

In league play that season Fostoria won two games from each of the following teams: Tiffin, Green Springs, Fremont, Monroeville, Fremont-Lynn, Clyde, Republic, Fort Seneca, and Millersville. Two records were established by the local tossers in league competition during the 1934 season. At Green Springs, they put up a new mark by tossing 456 single ringers, and at Fremont they made another new record by tossing 93 double ringers.

Members of the Fostoria Horseshoe Club pictured here, from left to right, are as follows: (front row) Al Daleski, C. Allison, John Saxton, H.A. Whitmore, Bob Whitman, K. Allison (secretary), and N. Fletcher; (middle row) Dwight Yates, W.K. Kunkelman, Art Dillon. A. Allison, (assistant manager), Wes Martin, and Harry Roth; (back row) C.L. Kunkelman (manager), Charles Yates (president), and K. Kunkelman.

JOHN B. ROGERS THEATER
(March 9, 1977)

A mixture of shock and regret must have filled Fostorians, as it did me a few weeks ago when the *Review Times* published the story about John B. Rogers Company closing their doors. John B. Rogers, the founder, as well as the company, was a part of this community for so many years I guess everyone thought it would always be. John B. Rogers productions have been known from coast-to-coast and outside of the United States borders. They were well known for staging revues, musical shows, pageants, and minstrels—and using home talent to whip up a good production in a few weeks.

There may have been many reasons for their success, but you know the old saying, "everyone wants to get into the act," and every participant usually had a particular talent to contribute. On top of that, the company always had capable directors to coordinate the talent and put the show together. Consequently, when the curtain went up on opening night of a John B. Rogers production, everyone knew their lines, their songs, the dance steps, and authentic costumes to fit the occasion had been fitted to the whole cast. If it happened to be a comedy or minstrel, the acts brought roars of laughter from the audience, and nearly rolled them in the aisles.

The company staged shows for service clubs, lodges, country clubs, junior-leagues—any group that wanted to raise funds. At one time, many years ago, the company had already set records of producing more than 20,000 shows in the United States and Canada, of raising more than $8 million for charitable organizations and had played 20 to 40 return engagements in many towns. The company had the largest staff of expert promoters, coaches, script and music writers, scenic and costume artists, and the greatest supply and equipment house in the world devoted exclusively to productions with amateurs.

John B. Rogers was attending the University of Michigan, studying law, when a previously injured eye became so seriously infected he was forced to discontinue his studies. He returned to Fostoria, depressed that he would not be able to continue his studies. According to a testimonial letter written by Andrew Emerine, president of Fostoria's First National Bank of that era, Rogers would often visit their house and put on stunts and skits, dressed up in Emerine's sister's clothes. He was reported a "riot." So, during his period of idleness, Rogers helped put on a show with home talent for the benefit of a local charity—just to pass the time. Owing to his hitherto undeveloped ability, it was a remarkable success. He was asked to repeat the performance in neighboring towns and thus the idea for his future company was born.

The John B. Rogers Producing Company was formed in 1903. The first location was on South Main Street, where Peggs Wallpaper and Paint Store is now. The company occupied the entire lower floor, while the upstairs had rented living quarters. It wasn't long before the company experienced "growing pains," and rented space in the Security Building to supplement their space needs. Then in 1926, they purchased land from the Auto-Lite Company for a new building at their present location on West Center Street and construction started immediately.

Harry Munsey, a young business man, operating a cigar store in Chicago, joined the company in 1911. He became a partner and remained with the company until 1962, when he died. John B. Rogers retired from the Company in 1945, wishing to enjoy a well-earned rest, and in 1946 sold his interest in the company to Harry Munsey. It was at that time that William E. "Bill" Munsey and W.W. Munsey joined the company. Bill Munsey has been president of the company for 16 years. John B. Rogers died in California and is buried there.

Pictured here is the John. B. Rogers Company location on West Center Street.

Shown here is the Rogers cast on stage.

KINSEY FAMILY TROUPERS
(February 1 and 8, 1979)

The world is made up of all kinds of people. Some like to be entertained, and others to entertain. There are the born actors, and those who prefer to be spectators. That natural combination made sports, movies, stage shows successful—and no less the traveling tent shows that were so popular in the latter part of the last century and through the first half of this century. Older Fostorians remember the Kinsey Komedy Kompany and the Madge Kinsey Players, which was an outgrowth of the former.

It was early in the summer of 1888 that M.L. Kinsey, a veteran actor for his 24 years, opened with his own repertoire company in Des Moines, Iowa. On the morning after the show's opening night a Des Moines paper had this to say: "The Kinsey's, now playing the opera house block for the week, is strictly a high-class company and the most refined may rest assured of a clean, model show. The people are all high-grade artists in their several parts; the specialty is exceedingly beautiful and fine." Young Kinsey took the paper's encouragement seriously, and moved eastward with his players, stopping in opera houses and town halls along the way, heading for New York City.

In the summer of 1901, he set up his first tent-theater in Shreve, Ohio, a small town south of Wooster. He must have liked Ohio, because Shreve was the headquarters for his players for a number of years, and only on a few occasions did his company go outside of Ohio. Each spring the show would leave town for its tour of week stands in the towns close enough to be reached by horse-drawn wagons that hauled the equipment. The actors traveled by train. When automobiles came into existence, trucks replaced the wagons and the actors used autos.

When the Kinsey Company was touring Michigan, M. Kinsey met and married Beth Hughes. The new Mrs. Kinsey was born into a non-theatrical family, but with the careful tutoring of her husband soon became the show's leading lady, and two successive generations followed in her footsteps and stayed with the popular tent-show. Frank F. Miller came to Kinsey's in 1900 as comedian and specialty artist. In 1907, M.L. Kinsey died and his wife Beth took over active management of the company. Later, she married Frank Miller and he took over managerial duties in the same style as M.L. Kinsey. In 1937, Beth Kinsey Miller retired from the company.

Fostoria was one of the Ohio towns that got on the Kinsey schedule back in the early 1900s. The show and the players made a hit here, and in later years Fostoria became winter headquarters. When the show broke up, Fostoria became the retirement town for many of the show's players. Otto "Toby" Imig and his wife, Esther, both associated with the popular Kinsey group for many years, have resided in Fostoria for many years. George Colbert and wife, Joanne, also part of the Kinsey cast, settled in Fostoria after leaving the show and were associated with John B. Rogers Company

The Kinsey presentations were varied. There was "Pollyanna," "Rebecca of Sunnybrook Farm," "Dottie Ray," "The Little Girl God Forgot," "Ten Nights in a Bar Room," "Within the Law," "Uncle Tom's Cabin," "Tempest and Sunshine," "St. Elmo," "The Millionaires Son and the Shop Girl," "Lena Rivers," "Our New Minister," "East Lynne"—and many more.

Madge Kinsey Graf, daughter of founder M. Kinsey and wife, Beth, was the moving force that kept the company going strong after the death of her parents, then later under the name of Madge Kinsey Players. Madge was a trouper all her life. She made her first stage appearance in swaddling cloths in her father's arms, doing the part in pantomime. The Madge Kinsey Players played their last show in 1954.

Playing the same towns year after year, the actors "boarded" in the same homes year after year creating a strong friendship between the players and the spectators. There were three generations of Kinsey players and three generations of friendly spectators.

The Kinsey Players pose in 1938, from left to right, as follows: (front row) the song and dance chorus line of Kathryn Fortner (Jemofsky), Mary Jane Davis (Bushkuhl), Bette Graf (Murdock), Esther Davis (Munsey), Jean Graf Graves, and Jewel Parsons with husband James; (middle row) E.H. Graf (owner-manager), Madge Kinsey Graf, Lottie Ansphach, George Colbert with wife Joanne, Eddie Mason with wife Babe, and Hugo Imig (father of "Toby"); (back row) Floyd Anspach (husband of Lottie) and Robert Merrick (both canvas and prop men), Mrs. Charles Graf (mother of Harry), Otto "Toby" Imig with wife Esther, and Dave Hemminger.

WILD WEST SHOWS
(June 10 and 24, 1982)

Remember Buffalo Bill Cody's Wild West Show, and the others similar to it, which amused and thrilled spectators with fancy horse riding, shooting, knife throwing, and roping? If you do, then you are an "old-timer," because Cody's show made its last appearance in 1917. But, perhaps you have heard someone from that era tell of the exciting performances of the Wild West shows that toured the nation, including Ohio, for many years.

Another one of the Wild West shows that toured Ohio after Cody's show had quit was "Montana Meechy's Real Wild West Show." It ran from 1924 to 1936. Its principle was "Edward Raymont Meech," better known as "Montana," who had been in the Cody show until it closed in 1917. Some Fostorians may remember Meechy since he and his band appeared at the Moose hall here on December 14, 1935.

When "Montana" and Myrtle Meech started their show in 1924, Myrtle did a shooting act. In 1929, she shot in competition with the famous Annie Oakley, to attempt to take her title away from her. Annie hit 98 and 97 out of 100 targets tossed into the air. Myrtle started her shooting act in her parent's show when she was only 4 years old and was 5 1/2 before she missed a shot.

When "Montana" and Myrtle decided to form their own show in 1924, he built his own show trucks on a side street in Columbus. They were square bodies on Ford truck chassis, painted orange and lettered in red. He also had a medicine show where a cure-all patent medicine was sold. The man and wife team would do an act to attract the crowd for sale of the medicine.

Taylor Brumbaugh, my wife's deceased uncle, who lived in Fostoria many years ago, substantiates that Cody was acquainted with Ohio, probably due to his show tours through the state. According to Brumbaugh, when he was a young man, Cody was in Fostoria at one time to see his old friend Frank Singer, who lived at 217 East Fremont Street, just west of the New York Central tracks. At that time, Brumbaugh was at the Singer home and held the reigns of the horse Cody had ridden there while the old friends visited. Presumably, Cody's show was not too far from Fostoria for Cody to ride there.

Annie Oakley was born August 13, 1860, near Greenville, Ohio. She was christened Phoebe Ann Oakley Mozee, but at some time the last name became Moses. Her parents were Quakers, who came from Pennsylvania. At 16, Annie out-shot Frank Butler, a talented marksman in a contest. Her skill so impressed him that within a year he married her. For the rest of their show career he was her manager. They were a part of Cody's show for 17 years as it toured the United States and Europe. Annie opened every show after the initial fanfare and grand entry.

According to one account, when the Sioux Indian chief Sitting Bull joined the show, he immediately took a great interest in Annie and admired her shooting. He called her "Little Sure Shot" and in a formal ceremony adopted her as his daughter. In England, Annie was presented to Queen Victoria. In Germany, during a special independent tour, Prince Wilhelm, later to become Kaiser Wilhelm, entered the arena while Annie was performing and requested her to repeat a feat he had seen her do in England. In this event, he held the lighted cigarette between his lips and Annie severed the lighted portion with a bullet from her rifle.

Earl L. Peter, residing at 105 East Eagle Street, told me that he was about nine years old when Cody brought his show to town in 1899. Peter recalls the stagecoach being chased around the show grounds by the whooping Indians, who in turn were chased off by Buffalo Bill and his band of rough riding cowboys.

Pictured here is "Montana" Meechy's Wild West Show in August of 1939.

"Montana" Meecy.

Annie Oakley.

PARKS AND BEACHES
(April 20, 1977; January 10, 1978; and March 9, 1978)

There were lots of places for families or couples on dates to go in the early days of the 1900s. Reeves and Meadowbrook parks were built to increase the traffic on the electric lines that served them. The TF&E (Tiffin, Fostoria & Eastern) served Tiffin, and Bascom where Meadowbrook is located. The TF&F (Toledo, Fostoria & Findlay) served Reeves Park at Arcadia. Reeves Park was located where Dicken Mfg. Company is now, at the north edge of Arcadia. Both parks offered ample picnic facilities and swings and slides for the kids. Both had dance floors in the pavilions and picnic areas for inclement weather. Reeves had the added inducement of bowling, roller-skating, and a baseball diamond.

The original Meadowbrook pavilion, shown in the photo, with its boardwalk, burned in 1925. It was rebuilt in 1933, but again burned, and the present pavilion was rebuilt in 1935. Reeves Park was named after Sam Reeves, President of the TF&F. The Reeves pavilion was struck by lightning and burned in the late 1920s. It was never rebuilt and the other buildings were later demolished.

At Riverside Park in Findlay you could picnic, swim, go boating, dance, or ride in the Steamer City of Findlay up the Blanchard River to the uptown area. Near Findlay on the Blanchard River is where Tell Taylor, who was born in Vanlue in 1876 and died in Chicago in 1937, penned the song "Down by the Old Mill Stream":

My darling I am dreaming, of the days gone by,
When you and I were sweethearts, beneath the summer sky;
Your hair has turned to silver, the gold has faded too;
But still I will remember where I first met you.
The old mill wheel is silent, and has fallen down,
The old oak tree has withered, and lies there on the ground;
While you and I are sweethearts, the same as days of yore;
Although we've been together, forty years or more.
Down by the old mill stream, where I first met you,
With your eyes of blue, dressed in gingham too,
It was there I knew, that you loved me true,
You were sixteen, my village queen, by the old mill stream.

There were other places in the Fostoria area that were not in the same class as Meadowbrook and Reeves Parks, but still frequented by the kids—especially boys. One such place was Woods Pond, where Gray Park is now, prior to the time George M. Gray purchased it. It was popular spot in summer for the boys to cool off with a dip in the water, even though muddy. In the wintertime it provided a place to ice skate.

One summer-time trip I will never forget is the boat ride from Toledo across Lake Erie to Canada on the steamer Greyhound. The steamer left the Toledo dock at about 8 a.m. and didn't get back until approximately 10 p.m. There were about two hours upon arrival at the Canadian port of Windsor to buy refreshments and souvenirs and to look around. With three decks on the steamer there were many nooks and crannies to explore and plenty of standing room along the railings to look out across the lake.

Lake Erie provided many popular beaches for swimming and picnics: Erie, Sandy, Gem, Terrace, and the very popular Cedar Point, to name a few. Still another popular place for the younger set was Rainbow Gardens at Fremont, where many of the Big Name Bands provided music for dancing. Older readers will never forget the Paramount Theatre, Toledo, with its beautiful lobby, its ornately decorated interior and—above all, the organ that could be elevated for musical presentations and the sing-a-long for the audiences. I would be remiss not to mention the Chautauqua programs held in the summertime. They were tent affairs, and brought to Fostoria, as they did to many communities, a variety of programs—musical, speakers, and plays.

Here is a view of Meadowbrook Park and Pavilion at Bascom.

Shown here is Reeves Park in Arcadia.

Pictured here is the steamship *Greyhound* on Lake Erie.

Here is a view of Fostoria Municipal swimming pool.

Five

SOME OUTSTANDING CITIZENS

C.C. ANDERSON
INDUSTRIALIST

(January 24, 1978)

September 1904, at the corner of Wood and North Streets, C.C. Anderson, Carl as he was generally known, established his C.C. Anderson Manufacturing Company to make muslin and flannelette undergarments. In 1905, a large addition was added and a similar plant was built at Findlay, Ohio, with plans to build plants at McComb and Kenton. The Anderson Mfg. Company had the distinction of being the largest cutter of muslin and flannelette garments in the world. Historical records of that day had this to say: "The buildings are roomy, airy, and women who do the work have every comfort of the parlor. Women are taken into this establishment, taught how to sew, and paid while they are learning. Three hundred people are employed in each factory."

The building later housed the Allen Motor Car Company, and still later the Hoyt Seed Company, which was located there just prior to the purchase by the YMCA for expansion purposes, at which time the building was demolished.

Anderson, who was rated as Fostoria's most influential and honored citizen at that time, was born in Bluffton, Ohio, on December 2, 1877. He was educated in the common school at Fremont, Ohio, and started life as a newspaper vender, later filling clerical positions in the offices of the L.S. & M.S. and L.E.&W. Railroads. Later he became a traveling salesman for the A.H. Jackson Mfg. Company, a manufacturer of undergarments, which was a competitor to him when he organized C.C. Anderson Mfg. Company (see the story on Jackson company on page 70).

Anderson's meteoric rise to fame was cut short by an early death at age 35. On October 1, 1912, Anderson with other associates was campaigning for re-election to that office, by visiting villages in this area. Returning to Fostoria on the New Riegel road that night, the car in which they were travelling had a tire blowout, which put them in the ditch, overturned, killing Anderson and injuring others.

Anderson was Mayor of Fostoria in 1905. Later he became Ohio Congressman for the 13th district. He was president of the local Board of Trade, president of Fostoria Hospital Association, a director of Seneca Wire and Mfg. Company, also the Blue Mfg. Company, president of the Mitchel Reversible Window Company, Fremont, and president of the Fostoria Baby Carriage Storm Shield Company. At the time of Anderson's death he planned to attend the National Democratic Convention in Chicago.

Shown here is the C.C. Anderson Manufacturing Company at Wood and North Streets, 1904.

WILLIAM W. CAMPBELL
ASTRONOMER

(August 2, 1979)

William Wallace Campbell was born on a farm in Hancock County, April 11, 1862. He had no recollection of his father, of Scottish descent, who died in 1866. The mother's task of raising of six children on the farm proved too much, so they moved to Fostoria. Wallace attended school in Fostoria and graduated in 1880 from old Central High. He expressed indebtedness to Miss Abbot, a high school teacher, who detected his abilities and urged him to attend a recognized university.

After teaching for two years, he acted on Miss Abbott's advice and applied for admission to the University of Michigan in 1882, in civil engineering. During his third year he found a copy of Simon Newcomb's "Popular Astronomy" at the library and read it through in two days and two nights. In later years, he told his friends that then and there he "discovered" astronomy and decided to make it his life-study. During his last year at the University he served as an assistant in the observatory. He graduated in 1886 with a bachelor of science degree. For two years after graduation, Campbell was professor of mathematics at University of Colorado. There he met Elizabeth Ballard Thompson, a student. They were married in 1892, shortly after becoming associated with Lick Observatory.

The Lick Observatory opened in 1888, and Professor Schaeberle resigned at U of M to join the new institution. Campbell was invited to take his old professor's job. In 1890, during summer vacation, Campbell served as a volunteer assistant at Lick Observatory, working under James E. Keeler on spectroscopic observations. When Keeler resigned, Campbell was invited to continue with Lick; he later was to be in charge of spectroscopic work.

The next thirty years of Campbell's life were spent with Lick and getting involved in many studies about the heavens, with some emphasis on eclipses. In 1922, a party headed by him traveled to the west coast of Australia to photograph an eclipse. Their desire was to get photographs that would permit him to measure the relativity deflection theory as it related to the gravitational deviation of light. When the results of their work were evaluated, they verified the values predicted by Einstein in the general theory of relativity. When Campbell returned from the Australian trip, he was offered the presidency of the University of California, which he accepted, but also retained directorship of Lick Observatory.

In 1931, he accepted an invitation to become president of the National Academy of Sciences in Washington D.C., an organization created by the Congress in 1863, which specified no duties other than that the academy would hold an annual meeting and should, "whenever called upon by any department of the government, investigate, examine and experiment, and report upon any subject of science or art."

On the conclusion of Campbell's term of office at the academy, he and Mrs. Campbell returned to California, making their home in San Francisco. His death occurred June 14, 1938. As might be expected, Campbell had many honorary degrees and filled many lectureships at various universities. He was also a member of many societies and organizations pertaining to science or astronomy. The Fostoria Board of Education offered to name the high school in his honor, but he declined.

William W. Campbell

FATHER JOHN E. DUFFY
WORLD WAR II CHAPLAIN

(March 27, 1986)

Father John E. Duffy, who was once on the staff of St. Wendelin and served as assistant to the Reverend R.V. O'Connor, was honored posthumously recently by the New London American Legion Post 292. The deceased Father Duffy was a survivor of the Bataan Death March during World War II.

Father Duffy was commissioned in the United States Army in 1933. After the Japanese attack on Pearl Harbor, he was ordered to the Philippines by General McArthur at the request of General Wainwright to be the Northern Luzon Force chaplain and later became chaplain of the First Philippine Corps, a position he held through the rest of his military career. When the Japanese overran Bataan, Father Duffy was forced to surrender and join the death march, during which he was bayoneted by the Japanese and left for dead. He was rescued by the Philippino guerillas and after recovering from his wounds directed guerrilla activities and cleared information in four provinces for Colonel Claud Thorpe, McArthur's guerilla chief.

Captured in 1943 by the Japanese, he was tried as a guerilla but not convicted. He is the only officer to ever beat a Japanese Kemptai court-martial. As a prisoner of war, he was forced to sail on the Japanese "Hell Ships." During one voyage he was wounded three more times. Although seriously wounded, he organized a relief party ministering to the dying and wounded. Of 17 chaplains who sailed with the Hell Ships, Father Duffy was one of only two who survived the ordeal.

At one point in his military career he was rescued by Philippinos and hidden in a Spanish hospital for four months while being treated for blood poisoning. He was forced to leave the hospital before the infection was cleared up because the Japanese had three times searched the hospital for him—the American who was alleged to have been there.

At another time Father Duffy discovered and took an American storm flag from a Japanese ammunition box. Wrapped on his person, it was never detected and later was turned over to Chaplain Wilcox, with instructions to send it to his niece if he should not survive. The flag finally arrived in the United States at the home of his niece in June of 1945 and was flown in the State of Ohio while he was still a prisoner in the Mukden POW hospital in Mukden, Manchuria, where he remained a patient of the Japanese until the end of the war.

Flown out of Manchuria on the first available plane because he was considered the most serious patient, he was at the general hospital three weeks; Calcutta General Hospital, three days; Walter Reed General Hospital for over a year, until he was officially retired on October 31, 1946.

Father Duffy's decorations, which are now permanently displayed in the showcase at the American Legion Post 292 in New London, include Legion of Merit, Bronze Star, Purple Heart with five oak leaf cluster, American Defense Medal with foreign service palm; Pacific Theater Medal with two battle stars; American Theatre ribbon; World War II Victory Medal; Philippine Defense Medal with one battle star; and Philippine Liberation Ribbon.

Father Duffy was ordained to the priesthood June 8, 1928, and was immediately sent to Fostoria. His teaching assignment at St. Wendelin included Latin, religion, and coaching of the debate team. He also organized the Wranglers Club, an organization of debators and orators. On May 15, 1930, after two years at St. Wendelin, he was transferred to St. Ann's Parish, Fremont.

Father Duffy's first and only civilian parish, serving as a priest, was Our Lady of Lourdes Church, New London, Ohio, which began in January 1947, after his release from military service.

Twice, Father Duffy was Commander of American Legion Post 292 at New London, 1947–48 and 1948–49. He was elected national chaplain of the American Legion at the National Convention in New York in 1952–53.

Father Duffy died June 4, 1958, in a United States hospital in San Francisco, at age 58, shortly after he had taken up residence at his retirement home in California. Father Duffy's final resting place is in Presidio National Cemetery, San Francisco, California. That cemetery is on a hill overlooking the city. The burial spot had been reserved for someone very special, and was designated for Father Duffy at the time of his death.

This 1930 "Froslin" photo shows Father John E. Duffy when he was at St. Wendelin.

DEAN C. EGER
WOOLWORTH EXECUTIVE

(July 5, 1979)

Dean Eger was born in a small community in northwestern Ohio called Pleasant Bend in the year 1896, to Charles A. and Lucy E. Eger. Pleasant Bend is still on the Ohio map, population 150, seven miles from Holgate on Ohio 115 in Henry County.

Dean's father had a general store in that farming community, and supplied the farmers with all the things they could not produce, in exchange for their products such as butter, eggs, chickens, and vegetables. It was a kind of barter system, which benefited both parties. If the farmer had a poor year with the crops, he traded what he could for necessities, or bought "on time," paying later, in cash or barter.

Eger had two "huckster wagons," which Dean's older brothers, Henry, Lewis, and George, took turns driving throughout the farming community carrying whatever the farmers needed, in exchange for produce. Dean remembers that as a young boy he could occasionally go along on the wagon trips with his brothers, stopping to have lunch at one of the farm homes. It was always a hospitable action on the part of farmers to feed those who happened by.

Undoubtedly he helped around the store with various chores, which had some bearing on his decision to enlist with F.W. Woolworth Company in later years. The writer has been acquainted with the Eger family for many years, and knows about their habits and qualities—hardworking, industrious, extremely faithful and devoted, honest—qualities that must have been ingrained in the parents and passed on to the Eger children.

In 1906, Dean's parents, with Dean and his two sisters, Carrie and Vera, moved to Fostoria. The three older brothers had already left Pleasant Bend for "greener pastures"; the brothers Lewis and George having migrated south, and Henry had already moved to Fostoria. Some of the Eger's furniture was shipped here in a railroad car. Some was brought in one of the huckster wagons, taking two days to make the 50-mile trip.

It was 1912, while attending Fostoria High School, that Dean started to work part-time for the local Woolworth store. Another of Dean's boyhood experiences here was to get a job carrying papers for the *Fostoria Daily Times*. One of Dean's boyhood friends who also carried the *Times* was Roscoe Fletcher Good, who later became an admiral in the Navy (See page 112). Dean recalls what a good boyhood friend Fletch was. While waiting for their papers they would often go to the Gerlinger Bakery at 209 North Main Street to buy a roll or cookie for a penny.

It was also 1912 when F.W. Woolworth and Company consolidated with S.H. Knox and Company, F.M. Kirby and Company, E.P. Carlton and Company, and W.H. Moore, to form F.W. Woolworth and Company, the giant merchandising company. And, it was 1912 that construction of the Woolworth Building in New York City was completed, the place where Dean Eger would finally land after 31 years, moving from one responsibility to another in his climb to the executive level as executive buyer.

Dean graduated from FHS in 1915. In September, he started to work for the Woolworth store in Findlay. Then he was transferred to Detroit, and later to Battle Creek, Michigan, where he stayed until being drafted into the Army in 1918. Upon being discharged in 1919, Dean worked for Woolworth in Toledo as assistant manager. He was store manager in 1920. He moved to Batavia, New York, as manager in 1921, then on to Binghamton, again as manager.

It was in 1927 that he was elevated to district manager of a group of stores and was moved to the regional offices in Buffalo, New York. When a new regional office was opened in Albany, in 1929, Dean was transferred there as district manager, a job he filled until 1936, when he was made a merchandise manager. He stayed in that position until 1946, when he moved into the slot he held until his retirement, executive buyer in the New York main office.

At a testimonial dinner when he retired in 1962, he was described as a man endowed with consideration for his friends and associates. His years of service are a tribute to outstanding loyalty, fairness, and integrity to all with whom he had contact.

In 1965, when Dean retired, he and his wife, Martha, moved from their home in Bronxville, New York, to Florida, where they have lived since. The Eger's had two sons and a daughter. Fostorians know Vera Eger, Dean's sister, as a respected and competent teacher in local schools for many years, as was another sister, Carrie.

Pictured above is the Eger's "huckster wagon" in front of their home on McDougal Street. Pictured at right is Dean C. Eger.

FRED T. FUGE
PREACHER AND WRITER

(October 25 and November 1, 1979)

Fred T. Fuge was born in 1872 in a tiny fishing village named Moretons Harbor, on the northeast coast of Newfoundland, into a family that had fished for a living for generations. As Fuge said in one of his many books, "From the time I was stout enough to crawl into calico breeches and handle a pair of paddles and cast a fishing-line, my place was in the hinder part of my father's boat."

As a boy, Fuge was converted to Christ in a "cottage" (home) church, which were sweeping that part of the country in the 1880s. When he was a young man he went to sea, making many foreign voyages. During those years he strayed from his earlier spiritual awakening, running from God. On one occasion on the high seas, he was working in the boiler room when the boiler exploded and set fire to the hold of the shop. His life endangered, Fuge called upon God to save him, and He did.

It was in the New York City harbor, where Fuge was unloading a cargo of sugar, that a sling broke and approximately 1,000 pounds of sugar fell on him. Crushed and unconscious he was rushed to a hospital, and he remembers calling on God again for help. After a long period of recovery he returned to his home in Newfoundland. He now felt the strongest call of his life to do something for God. He started working with the Salvation Army. His next move was to God's Bible School at Cincinnati, where he stayed for some time.

From God's Bible College he came to Fostoria in the early 1900s and started a small mission church. Under his guidance, that group later built the Independent Holiness Church at Liberty and Union Streets, now used by the Bethel United Methodist Church. In later years, Fuge recalled that in those early days it was not a problem to get people to go to church, "Often I had difficulty reaching the pulpit because people filled the aisles."

After pastoring that church for some time, Fuge and his wife and daughter went to Africa as missionaries where they served for 20 years. When he was 87, he admitted that his heart was still with the Zulu tribe in Africa, and the only thing that kept him from going back was his "old body."

Sometime after returning to Fostoria from Africa, Fuge became the second pastor to serve the Nazarene Church in Fostoria. Fuge also started and pastored several other small independent churches in Fostoria. I am told by Fostorian Lance Marshall, one of his old friends, that when he preached he gripped and held the audience's attention like all great orators. He never used a note for reference, but spoke from knowledge and memory.

F. T. Fuge passed away in July of 1968 at the age of 96 and is buried in Fostoria Fountain Cemetery. He was not known by the greater populace of Fostoria, yet had sailed the oceans of this globe, spent 20 years in Africa, and spread the message of the Bible wherever he went. He also wrote at least 30 books and booklets on various subjects during his lifetime.

Reverend Fred T. Fuge.

110

ROBERT LOCKHART
REAR ADMIRAL, U.S. NAVY

(April 13, 1978)

Robert Green Lockhart was born in Fostoria on January 10, 1902, to John W. and Laura (Green) Lockhart. Older Fostorians will remember his father, John, as a former owner of the *Fostoria Review*, and, after its sale, as news editor of the *Daily Times*. The Lockhart family lived at 223 West Tiffin Street. The house still stands, unaltered, but now painted red, and occupied by the Donald Watkins family.

"Bob" Lockhart, as he was known to Fostorians, graduated from Fostoria High School in 1919. He was vice president of his high school class, and on the *Red and Black* staff. Opposite his photo in the *Red and Black Annual* appeared the quote: "I want to be a sailor, a sailor, a sailor." And so he became—and notably too!

He graduated from the United States Naval Academy in 1924. He received aviation training at the Naval Base at Pensacola, Florida; and subsequently was stationed at many bases around the United States and in other countries. Lockhart was a lieutenant commander aboard the battleship *West Virginia* and was a member of the admiral's staff at Pearl Harbor at the time of the infamous attack by the Japanese.

During World War II, he was serving as navigation officer on the ill-fated *Hornet* when she was bombed and disabled after a suicide attack by Japanese dive bombers and torpedo planes in the South Pacific, east of the Solomon Islands in October 1942. Lockhart and Rear Admiral Charles P. Mason were the last two men to abandon the *Hornet*. Two months earlier, the *Hornet* was used by Jimmy Doolittle's bombers for their attacks on Japan.

He was named executive officer of the Alameda (California) Naval Air Base after the sinking of the Hornet. Later he was promoted to the rank of captain and was named commander of the United States Navy Air Training Field, Olathe, Kansas. At the close of the war, Lockhart became naval attaché to the United States Embassy in Copenhagen, Denmark, where he remained until 1955, after which he was retired from the Navy with rank of admiral, having served his country for 36 years.

Pictured here are Rear Admiral and Mrs. Lockhart when they lived in Copenhagen, Denmark.

ROSCOE FLETCHER GOOD
ADMIRAL, U.S. NAVY

(January 11, 1979)

Admiral Good was Fostoria's highest ranking naval officer. He also attained the honor of serving in two world wars as well as the Korean conflict. Many other service honors were awarded him in the 42 years that he served his country. "Fletch" Good, as he was known to many Fostorians, was born in Fostoria March 13, 1897, and graduated from Fostoria High School in 1914. For two years after graduation he was a reporter and advertising solicitor for the *Fostoria Daily Times*.

In 1916, Good received an appointment to the United States Naval Academy. Before he completed his training there he was drafted into service during World War I in 1919 and served for six months aboard the USS *Wyoming* and USS *New Jersey*, as part of the Atlantic fleet. He was returned to the Academy to graduate with his class in 1920, standing fourth in a class of 452. He was editor of his class paper, "Lucky Bag."

His marriage to Bess Louise Owen, a Fostoria girl, took place August 2, 1919, aboard the USS *Columbia*, the ship to which he was assigned for three years after graduation from the Academy. After that he had submarine training and was assigned to the USS *O-12* in August 1921. His sea duty continued as Commanding Officer of USS *L-9* and Executive Officer, USS *S-21*. In 1922, he was Commanding Officer USS *S-17* in Panama.

In June of 1924, "Fletch" began postgraduate instruction in diesel engineering in Annapolis and continued at Columbia University, from which he received his MS degree in 1926. Good had three more years of submarine duty before reporting to Bureau of Engineering. From 1930 to 1932 he was submarine superintendent at the New York Navy Yard. He then joined Sub Division 10 in the USS *S-37* until May 1935 in the Far East. After two years as Officer-in-Charge of the Internal Combustion Engine Laboratory at the Naval Engineering Experimental Station, Annapolis, he reported for duty as navigator of the USS *Arkansas*.

Admiral Good served on the USS *Tuscaloosa* for a year before joining the staff of Commander Cruise Battalion Force in June 1939. In February of 1941, he transferred to the staff of Commander-in-Charge of Pacific Fleet as Assistant Operations Officer, stationed in Hawaii. He received the Legion of Merit for service in that capacity. In August 1943, Good reported for staff duty with Commander-in-Charge United States Fleet and Chief of Naval Operations. In October of 1944, he was assigned to the USS *Washington* and took command of her the following month. For meritorious conduct in battle in that command he was awarded a Gold Star in lieu of the second Legion of Merit with Combat "V," and a letter of commendation with ribbon.

Admiral Good became Commander of Cruiser Division Six in July 1945. In November of that year he reported to the Office of Chief of Naval Operations as head of the Fleet Operation (Logistics), stationed in Germany. Three years later (1956) he reported as Commander Naval Forces Far East (later Japan).

Admiral Good retired on March 1, 1956, and settled in Foley, Alabama, where several other naval officer friends also lived. As a civilian he was a civil and mechanical engineer. He had expected to do some fishing and enjoy retirement, but his health failed and he and his wife were forced to move to McLean, Virginia, where he died in February of 1973 at Bethesda Naval Hospital. He was buried with full military honors in Arlington Cemetery. First Lieutenant Roscoe F. Good III, the only child of the Goods, was killed in action in Korea, 1951.

The last participation of Admiral Good in public ceremonies in this area was in 1954, in Toledo, for Armed Forces Day. For that event he was introduced by Rear Admiral R.W. Carey, USN (Retired), holder of the Congressional Medal of Honor. Good's remarks at that event were not a speech, but a report on "Power for Peace," in which he described how the nation's defenses were being modernized to keep abreast of the needs for the future, when sabotage and air attack would be possible in the event of total war. Present at the Toledo meeting, with Admiral Good and his wife, were his four sisters, Mrs. W.D. (Kate) Kuhn, Mrs. Harvey Roth, Mrs. Harold (Doris) Buck, and Mrs. Lucy Bowe and two brothers-in-laws, W. D. Kuhn and Harold Buck. Other Fostorians present at the Toledo ceremonies were Mr. and Mrs. E.M. Hopkins and Mr. and Mrs. Harry Stoneberger.

Admiral Roscoe Fletcher Good

U.G. LEEDY
DRUM MAKER

(October 1, 1981)

Few Fostorians know that U.G. (Lester) Leedy, who became the organizer and president of the most famous drum manufacturing company in the world, lived in Fostoria when he was a boy. Back in 1874, when Leedy was only seven, he bought his first drum from a Civil War drummer who lived near Fostoria. At that time the Leedy family home was at 602 South Main Street, just a block away from the Baltimore and Ohio Railroad station. Just about train time, the story goes, the seven-year-old drummer would sit on the front doorstep and beat his drum, which was almost as big as he. His drumming entertained the passers-by, and many a penny or nickel was tossed his way.

By the time he was 14 years old young Lester had joined the 15th Regimental Drum Corps in Ohio and played with them, as well as at numerous political campaign entertainments. By the time he was 18, he was a full-fledged drummer with the Fostoria town band and orchestra.

It was in the 1880s, while he was playing an Arbor Day engagement in Fostoria, in which he was billed as a xylophone solo with the band, that the business manager of Cedar Point happened to be in town. He heard the concert and a few days later wrote to Leedy and asked him to substitute in the Great Western Band, at that time one of the country's leading bands, which was to play at Cedar Point. The young drummer was rather hesitant to take the job, as the drummer whose place he was taking was Max A. Wintrich, a fine drum artist who later was principal drummer in the Chicago Symphony Orchestra for 32 years. However, he finally accepted the engagement and soon became a featured member of the band on drums and xylophone.

Theatrical engagements rapidly followed, and Leedy did much traveling with minstrel shows, musical shows, and circuses. From his travels and his many contacts with drummers, he decided that there was a great need for better drummers' instruments.

He had been experimenting for some time with the construction of a stand to hold the snare drums, to get away from the unsatisfactory method of playing the drum on a chair. In 1890, while he was playing with a theater orchestra in Toledo, he finally invented and patented the first practical folding snare drum stand.

It was in the same year, 1890, that Leedy made his first drum. His father, a carpenter, made and shaped the solid wood shells to his son's specifications. Buying rods, heads, and snare strainers from various manufacturers, Leedy assembled and sold his first snare drum.

Shortly afterwards, he accepted a theater position in Indianapolis, where he continued his sideline activity of making drums, getting the wood shells from his father still living in Fostoria, and assembling the drums in the basement of his Indianapolis home. His position in the theater brought him into contact with many traveling drummers who became interested in the drums he made, and they placed orders with him. In time, orders for drums were coming from drummers all over the country, and the sideline business began to take up so much of his time and effort that Leedy decided to discontinue his theater work and devote his full time to making drummers' instruments.

In 1895, he and Sam Cooley, a clarinet player in the same theater orchestra, each put $50 into the business and began the manufacture of Leedy drums under the name Leedy Manufacturing Company. The first factory was a single room in the old Cyclorama Building in Indianapolis. From the very first the new firm prospered, and soon Leedy drums were being shipped to all parts of the country.

Other instruments were added to the line, and in 1902 Herman Winterhodd, an accomplished cello and trombone artist, who had also played in the theater orchestra with Leedy, joined the firm and took charge of the tuning of bells and xylophones.

The rapidly increasing demand for Leedy drummers' instruments necessitated a move to larger quarters. Land was bought at the corner of Barth Avenue and Palmer in Indianapolis. A 1-story building was constructed to house the expanding business. Continued growth required more manufacturing space, and by 1927 the Leedy factory comprised 78,450 square feet in a modern 30-story structure at the original location.

In 1929, control of the Leedy Company was acquired by C.G. Conn Ltd., and in 1930, the factory and personnel were moved to Elkhart, Indiana. Conn continued ownership until the late 1950s, when the Leedy name was purchased by the Singlerland Drum Company. When Leedy's corporation was at its peak they furnished instruments for most of the great bands and orchestras, including the Army, Navy, and Marine Bands.

One of the "Biggest" accomplishments of the Leedy Drum Company was construction in the 1920s of the first "monster" bass drum for Purdue University's marching band. It is still in use, and many readers may have seen it while attending football games, or on television.

Kermit and Lynn Leedy, who still live in the Fostoria area, are related to U.G. Leedy.

U.G. Leedy

Shown here is the large Purdue University drum made by Leedy, who is third from the left.

LEE MOORE
J.C. PENNEY VICE PRESIDENT

(March 23, 1977)

J. (James) C. (Cash) Penney started his business in 1902. He was one of those rugged, farsighted businessmen who started things moving in this country at the turn of the century. A devout Christian, he started in a very meager way and piloted his first store, and succeeding ones, to become a giant in the merchandising field. On April 27, 1918, the J.C. Penney Company opened a store in Fostoria. Last year (1976) Lee Moore, who had started working in the Fostoria store as a young man, moved up to the job as executive vice president of the Penney organization in the New York City office.

The Fostoria Penney store was one of the early group of stores opened by the company. Fostoria was selected because it was still an up-and-coming town, even though the gas-boom days had passed. The local store was the 187th in the chain, and the third Penney store east of the Mississippi River. E.R. "Ernie" Kellogg was the first manager, coming here from Kalispell, Montana. His ability, coupled with the wide variety of merchandise offered, made the store a beehive of activity. As a boy of that era I remember how the store was so crowded with customers, especially on Saturdays, that it was sometimes difficult to elbow your way through.

Mr. Kellogg was a devout Christian in the local Presbyterian Church. He was a tither, and after he had gained considerable wealth he distributed large amounts of his money for the support of church-related activities. In his later years he supported missionaries all over the world. He had hoped to live long enough to see Jesus' Second Coming, a wish unfulfilled. During the intervening years since Mr. Kellogg's time there have been five managers of the local Penney store. It was under Ralph "Red" Cummings, who had started under Mr. Kellogg, that Lee Moore started his career with the Penney organization, which eventually landed him in the New York office as executive vice president.

Moore began as an extra in the Fostoria store in 1940, three years after graduating from Fostoria High School as valedictorian. He became a full-time sales person four months later at Troy, Ohio, under Paul Jacoby, who had been assistant manager under Cummings. After a long tour of duty with the United States Army Air Force in World War II, and another three years as a salesperson, Moore moved up to floor manager at Cincinnati in 1950. Two years later he was manager of his own store in St. Louis, Missouri, and capturing the eyes of the corporate talent scouts from Penney headquarters in New York City. Moore is credited with reversing the downward trend of the Sarma-Penney Ltd. operations in Belgium and making it highly successful.

Last year, at age 57, and after 35 years with J.C. Penney, he was called back to the United States to become executive vice president succeeding Walt Meppl, who moved up to the job of president. Moore, in a letter to M.J. "Mike" Sabol, present manager of the Fostoria store, said, "Back in 1940, Fostoria was very much a 'Saturday town' . . . and bib overalls were our best-selling fashion item. There was a warm relationship between Penney's and the townspeople. Ralph Cummings was a good manager and a responsible citizen of his community. Thus you can understand my warm feelings for what is now your town." I don't know if Mr. Penney, the founder of the company, made it a point to visit all of the stores in the chain, but he did visit the Fostoria store during Cummings management, and Mrs. Kintz and Mrs. Sanders, employees at that time remember the occasion, as do others.

Lee Moore and his wife, Pat, live in Connecticut, with their pampered Great Dane dog, Lady Guinevere.

Store employees in 1954, during 35th Anniversary Sales Days, are pictured here, from left to right, as follows: (front row) Virginia Mann, Esther (Bare) Johnson, Mrs. Ruth Bare, Florence (Rowe) Kuhn, Blanche Bowman, Florence Sanders, Leota (Kiser) Solether, Mary (Howard) Kintz, Annabelle (Biggs) Fontaine, and Cleo Hull; (back row) Lyle B. Shaw, Cloyd Lott, Ralph Cummings (manager), Paul Jacoby (assistant manager), Leonard Skonecki, and Wade Lowe.

DAVID M. SCHLATTER
LIEUTENANT GENERAL, U.S. AIR FORCE

(January 26, 1989)

This is about General David M. Schlatter, the older brother of General George Schlatter (see page 119). For four years he was a flying instructor at Brooks Field and March Field, California. He was reassigned to France Field, Panama Canal Zone, and thereafter resumed duties as flying instructor at March Field and Randolph Field, Texas. David Schlatter graduated from Air Corps Tactical School, Maxwell Field, Alabama, and was transferred to Godman Field, Fort Knox, Kentucky, as an operations and intelligence officer. After graduating from the Command and General Staff School at Fort Leavenworth, Kansas, he was assigned to the advanced flying school at Keloy Field as Director of Flying and then moved to Moffett Field, California, as Director of Training of the West Coast Air Corps Training Center, serving later as Executive and Chief of Staff.

In February of 1942, he was assigned to Army Air Forces Headquarters in Washington as Director of Air Support. A year later, he became Deputy Chief of Staff of Air Training Command at Fort Worth, Texas. In September of 1943, when promoted to brigadier general, he was attending the Army and Navy Staff College. The following January, he was designated Deputy Chief of Staff for Operations of the Ninth Air Force in the European Theater.

On establishment of Supreme Headquarters, Allied Expeditionary Forces in Paris in October of 1944, he was assigned as Deputy Chief of Air Staff, and Commanding General of the United States Strategic Air Forces in Europe. His promotion to major general occurred in January of 1945.

Returning from Europe in late 1945, General Schlatter's initial assignment was to develop plans for the creation of a post-war career officer school system for the Army Air Force. He was the school's first acting commander and later the Deputy Commanding General for education of what later became known as the Air Force's Air University. In 1950, he organized and was first commander of Air Research and Development Command.

In 1951, General Schlatter returned to Europe to organize and become first commander of the North

Atlantic Treaty Organization's Allied Air Forces, Southern Europe. In that assignment, he was promoted to Lieutenant General in 1952. General Schlatter returned from Europe to take command of the Armed Forces Staff College in July 1954, and served in that position until his retirement due to physical disability on July 31, 1957.

The General and Mrs. Schlatter then settled in San Antonio, Texas, where he engaged in voluntary civic duties with Christ Episcopal Church, United Fund, Symphony Society of San Antonio, and others. His United States decorations included the distinguished Service Medal with Oak Leaf cluster, Legion of Merit, Bronze Star, and Air Medal. His many foreign decorations include honors from Great Britain, France, Greece, Italy, and the Netherlands. General Schlatter passed away on December 14, 1973.

General and Mrs. Schlatter are shown here in Florence, Italy, while he was NATO's first Commander of Allied Air Forces, Southern Europe.

GEORGE F. SCHLATTER
BRIGADIER GENERAL, U.S. AIR FORCE

(September 14, 1978)

Brigadier General George Fletcher Schlatter was born in Fostoria, November 25, 1905. He came from a well-liked and respected Fostoria family that resided at the southwest corner of Center and Wood Streets. His father, George, and uncle, Dan Schlatter, operated a meat market in Fostoria for many years on North Main Street. In high school George Schlatter took college prep courses and was active in band, orchestra, the debate team, and the senior class play. He graduated from Fostoria High School in 1925.

Mr. Schlatter attended Ohio Wesleyan University in 1926 for one-half year before entering the United States Military Academy at West Point. He graduated from West Point with a bachelor of science degree in 1930 and was commissioned a second lieutenant in the United States Army.

General Schlatter received his wings at Kelly Field, Texas, in October 1931. His Air Force career for the next 10 years was principally as a fighter pilot at Selfridge Field, Michigan, and as a flying instructor and flight commander at Randolph Field, Texas, and Maxwell Field, Alabama. Assigned to the Office of the Chief of the Air Corps in Washington D.C., in May 1941, General Schlatter served there as chief of pilot training during the fateful days of the beginning of World War II.

There followed a tour of duty in the Air Force Flying Training Command at Fort Worth, Texas, and assignment as Commandant at Stewart Field, flight facility for the United States Military Academy at West Point. For his outstanding work during the period from February of 1942 through March of 1943, which was the time of the great and rapid expansion of the Army Air Forces, General Schlatter was awarded the Legion of Merit.

General Schlatter's overseas World War II assignment was with the Twelfth Tactical Air Command in Europe, where he served as chief of staff. During his wartime duty, although a senior staff officer, the general flew 15 combat missions in F-47 fighter aircraft on dive bombing sorties and fighter sweeps with various units of the 12th TAC. This won him the Air Medal and the Distinguished Unit Badge.

Following his return to the United States in 1947, General Schlatter served at Randolph Air Force Base until his selection in 1948 to attend the National War College, where he graduated in 1949. His next assignment, bringing into play his early science and engineering training, was to the military staff of the Atomic Energy Commission, where he served as chief of the full-scale weapons test activities for three years. The Nevada test site was organized and Eniwetok Proving Ground was built during his tour of duty.

From 1952 to 1953, he was staff director of all flying and technical training for the Air Force during the Korean expansion. In 1955, the general was named Commander of the 2nd Air Division and chief of the military assistance advisory group in Saudia Arabia. In this assignment, he covered the entire Middle East with his transport crews, supplying other United States MAAG's and missions.

In 1960, he retired after more than 35 years of military duty as cadet and officer. General Schlatter and his wife, Eleanor, retired to Melbourne, Florida, where they were active in St. John's Episcopal Church.

General George Schlatter

DR. HAROLD YOCHUM
EDUCATOR

(August 3, 1978)

Born on a farm on McDougal Road, east of Fostoria, to W.H. and Ida Yochum, Harold, as well as his two sisters, received their early education at the Punk Hollow one-room school. Harold completed his first eight grades in six years. Yochum was a salutatorian of his graduating class at Fostoria High in 1919.

After graduating from Fostoria High School, Yochum entered Capital University, graduating in 1923 with a bachelor's degree. He received a master's degree from Ohio State in 1924, and bachelor of divinity degree from Evangelical Lutheran Theological Seminary in 1928. His early teaching experience was at Attica, where he was a teacher and high school principal in 1924–25. Then he returned to Capital University to teach English and Latin until 1928. Later he was pastor of Emmanuel Lutheran Church in Hesseville, and after that pastor of Holy Trinity Lutheran Church in Detroit. From 1937 to 1946 he was president of the Michigan district of the American Lutheran Church.

Dr. Harold Leland Yochum served as the ninth president of Capital University, Columbus, from 1946 until a retirement in 1969. During his 23-year tenure as president, the university tripled its enrollment and faculty; more than doubled the size of its campus; and added two professional schools, law and nursing, to its College of Arts and Sciences.

Throughout his entire career Dr. Yochum was dedicated to many educational and civic involvements. He was vice president of the Columbus Area Council of Churches from 1951–64 and was a delegate of the American Lutheran Church to attend meetings of the World Council of Churches in this country and overseas. He was chairman of the Franklin County United Appeal in 1963; a past president of the Ohio College Association; a past chairman of the Ohio Foundation of Independent Colleges; and past president of the Association of Independent Colleges and Universities of Ohio.

In 1950, when Capital University celebrated its centennial, Dr. Yochum had this to say about the University's future:

We believe that our objectives should be stated in terms of personality, rather than vague generalities and high-sounding ideals. What kind of person do we hope to graduate? One who is in right relationship with his total environment. . . an intergrated personality, living in fellowship with God and man, alert to current trends of thinking, standards of value, norms of judgment, be able to choose what is sound and reject what is fallacious. We best fulfill our obligations to church and society if our graduates are characterized by right attitudes and motivations, by intelligent ways of thinking and making decisions, by gracious ways of living and an appreciation of our entire cultural heritage. At the center of this will be a vital Christian faith and a reflection of that faith in character and life.

Dr. Harold L. Yochum

120

Six

Biblical and Patriotic Exhortations

Paul Krupp ended his "Potluck" columns with a Biblical or patriotic exhortation. Some folks considered this the best part of the column. Rather than include them with the edited articles, we have included a few select ones here in this chapter. We hope you enjoy them as much as did the original readers.

WHAT'S SO GREAT ABOUT AMERICA

(January 2, 1987)

This week's article, another in the series "The Rebirth of America," was written by Rus Walton, the executive director of Plymouth Rock Foundation, of Marlborough, New Hampshire. The foundation's main objective is "to advance the kingdom of the Lord, Jesus Christ."

In an exchange of correspondence to get Walton's permission to reprint the article, he commented, "Many thanks for sending me tearsheets of your column from the *Review Times*. If only we had more works such as yours in papers across the nation, perhaps we could lift the United States out of the morass of immorality which now degrades its standards and infests its institutions."

Half the world goes to bed hungry. And half the world lies under Communist rule, where freedom, as Americans know it, simply does not exist. Homemakers in much of the world might never see in a lifetime the quantity of food which the American housewife can choose in just one trip to the supermarket. Is this abundance and this freedom ours merely by chance? Is it wholly due to what Americans like to perceive as American energy and know how? If God indeed has blessed America, why?

One of our most moving patriotic hymns cites the beauty of America—a beauty that all who have traveled across the continent surely recognize. Kathlerine Lee Bates stood atop Pike's Peak and scanned the sweep of the land, then wrote of the "purple mountain majesties, and the amber waves of grain." She concluded that God has shed His grace on this land—a vast unexplored wilderness that, in an astonishingly short period, grew into a great nation.

It would be foolish to deny that the rich natural resources of the land itself have not helped to make America. The oil, the ore, the timber, the water, the soil and climate, all have combined to nourish a civilization that would eventually spread from sea to shining sea. Other nations too, though, have been blessed with fine resources, yet somehow these have not risen to such greatness.

Others have said that America's people have made her great. Lyman Abott once said, "A nation is made great, not by its mines, but by the men who build and run them. America was a great land when Columbus discovered it; Americans have made it a great nation." And so they have: they pioneered a continent, subdued the elements that at first worked against them, and molded a society of peoples from all over the world. America's initiative and ingenuity are known across the earth. Other nations have looked on in awe at her ability over the decades to produce not only her own needs, but much more.

America's free enterprise system and the spirit of her people, it would seem, have combined to deliver a flood of mass-produced goods to the consumer at relatively low cost. At the same time, American economic genius has also helped to produce millions of jobs, from the factories to the professions, which have given Americans the income to buy the goods they produce. Thus far America has escaped the specter of wide-scale hunger at home, and she has been able to feed at least some of the hungry abroad. Through the decades she has opened her heart to the poor of the world. She has given generously to every nation, even her enemies, in the time of emergency.

In spite of certain social ills, the United States of America has passed more social legislation and enacted more laws providing individual liberty than any other nation in world history. And because of her belief in freedom of speech she has not hidden her scars—they are there for the world to see—while those totalitarian regimes that run a controlled press look on amazed.

All of those blessings point back to her foundations and to the Providential hand of God. After all, the purple mountain majesties and the fruited plains originated with God. America's blessings, despite her ills, call forth thanksgiving from all those who enjoy them. The great spiritual heritage that built America unfolded by remarkable design. So also did American democracy, the United States Constitution, and along with these, the great freedoms they ensure. No, America did not just happen by chance, as is obvious to a person who truly understands the unfolding saga of events that shaped this nation. As

122

Thomas Jefferson once asked, "Can the liberties of a nation be secure, when we have removed the conviction that these liberties are the gift of God?"

"AMERICA, THE BEAUTIFUL"

O beautiful for spacious skies,
For amber waves of grain,
For purple mountain majesties
Above the fruited plain!
America! America!
God shed His grace on thee,
And crowned thy good with brotherhood,
From sea to shining sea!

Katherine Lee Bates

"Our laws and our institutions must necessarily be based upon and embody the teachings of The Redeemer of mankind. It is impossible that it should be otherwise, and in this sense and to this extent our civilization and our institutions are emphatically Christian . . . This is a religious people. This is historically true. From the discovery of this continent to the present hour, there is a single voice making this affirmation . . . we find everywhere a clear recognition of the same truth . . . These, and many other matters which might be noticed, add a volume of unofficial declarations to the mass of organic utterances that this is a Christian nation."

Supreme Court decision, 1892.
Church of the Holy Trinity v. the United States of Amercia.

PROVIDENCE SPRING STILL FLOWING
(May 4, 1978)

Most readers know something about the terrible Civil War in this country that set the North against the South, having studied it in school history courses or having heard certain stories of it passed on by parents or grandparents.

One such story was mentioned to me by Fostorian Blake Myers sometime ago. It concerned Providence Spring, the flowing spring of water that turned the tide when Northern soldiers were dying by the score every day because of sickness caused in part because of impure water. Myers' story set me researching, and I finally visited the site of Providence Spring at Andersonville, Georgia, where Northern prisoners were held during that tragic war.

Let's start at the beginning. Andersonville, the largest and best known of Southern military prisons was located in Sumpter County, Georgia, a station on the Southwestern Railroad (now Central of Georgia) nine miles northeast of Americus. It was selected as a prison site because Confederate officials foresaw the need to move Northern prisoners from Richmond and other prisons farther north in the event of a breakthrough by Southern forces. They felt it would be easier to guard them in a remote area. The new prison site was also selected because of the close proximity of the railroad, the presence of plenty of pure water, and warmer climate.

Confederate soldiers and slaves from nearby plantations began clearing the land and constructing the camp in January of 1864. In February, before the prison was near completion, 500 Northern troops arrived. Soon more prisoners were arriving at the rate of 400 per day. By August, 32,000 Northern soldiers were incarcerated in the 26-acre camp that was meant to hold 10,000. In addition to overcrowding, there was inadequate shelter, food, doctors, and means for treating the sick and injured.

Mostly, the prisoners had to construct their own shelters from whatever scrap materials they could find. Many prisoners had clothing that was in tatters, and often they were naked. Food was rationed meagerly and left to the prisoners to cook. Those who had money could buy food from the prison sutler and other merchants who had set up shops inside the stockade.

The stream of water that supplied the camp soon became polluted by human wastes and other pollutants. Diarrhea and dysentery spread throughout the camp. Deaths from those ailments, as well as from gangrene and other diseases, occurred by the scores—the greatest toll being 90 on August 23, 1864.

A group of Christian prisoners finally decided they would pray to God for pure water and would not stop until their prayers were answered. They prayed for hours—and then finally a deafening noise like thunder or an earthquake shook the earth, and where they were kneeling a stream of water burst forth from the ground. They considered this phenomenon a providential act of God, and so the stream of water was called Providence Spring. Blake Myers' grandfather was one of those in the prayer group and that is the story he told Blake when he was a boy, anxious to hear his grandfather's stories. Providence Spring has continued to flow all these years since 1864 and was flowing the day I saw it in March of this year.

A powerful Union force, under General James H. Wilson, captured Columbus, Georgia, on April 17, 1865, and shortly thereafter all Northern prisoners at Andersonville were freed. The prison grounds reverted to private ownership, but after the war were purchased by the Grand Army of the Republic (GAR) in 1890. The GAR and its auxiliary, the Women's Relief Corps, made many improvements to the old prison site. Clara Barton, the famous Civil War nurse, helped to identify and mark the graves of those who died at Andersonville. Additional interments, including the remains of Union soldiers originally buried in other Southern prison camps, were later moved to Andersonville, and today there are 13,669 marked graves at the National Cemetery, including 1,065 from Ohio. This cemetery, now comprising 84 acres, was administered by the United States Department of the Army until 1970, at which time it was turned over to the National Park Service.

The Women's Relief Corps in 1901 donated the pavilion that houses Providence Spring, in memory of those who died at Andersonville. A plaque inside the building reads: "This pavilion was erected by The Women's Relief Corp, Auxiliary to the Grand Army of the Republic, in grateful memory of the men who suffered and died in the Confederate prison at Andersonville, Georgia, from February 1864 to April 1865. The prisoners' cry of thirst rang up to Heaven, God heard, and with His thunder cleft the earth, and poured his sweetest waters gushing here."

The Graves of 13,669 Union soldiers rest at Andersonville, Georgia.

Pictured above is the Building housing Providence Spring, which is still flowing.

Rejoice in the Wonder of
Our Savior's Birth
(December 22, 1983)

The first six letters of Christmas—CHRIST—spell the real meaning of the day and the season which we are in. On the 25th of December we will be celebrating the most important day in world history. Nearly 2,000 years ago a baby boy was born to a Jewish man and woman, Joseph and Mary, and he was named Jesus. (Scholars have determined that He was actually born in September or October, but we celebrate His birth on December 25.)

Isaiah, the prophet, foretold 700 years earlier of that important event: "Therefore the Lord Himself will give you a sign: Behold a virgin shall conceive, and bear a Son, and shall call His name Immanuel." (Isaiah 7:14) And in Isaiah 9:6-7: "For unto us a Child is born, unto us a Son is given; and the government will be upon his shoulder. And His name will be called Wonderful, Counselor, Mighty God, Everlasting Father, Prince of Peace. Of the increase of his government and peace there will be no end, upon the throne of David and over His kingdom, to order it, and to establish it with judgment and with justice from that time forward, even forever."

Then much later, St. Matthew tells us, in Chapter 1, verse 18:

Now the birth of Jesus Christ was as follows: after His mother Mary was betrothed to Joseph, before they came together, she was found with child of the Holy Spirit. Then Joseph her husband, being a just man, and not wanting to make her a public example, was minded to put her away secretly. But while he thought about these things, behold, an angel of the Lord appeared to him in a dream, saying, 'Joseph, son of David, do not be afraid to take to you Mary your wife, for that which is conceived in her is of the Holy Spirit. And she will bring forth a Son, and you shall call his name Jesus, for He will save His people from their sins.' Then Joseph, being aroused from sleep, did as the angel of the Lord commanded him, and took to him his wife, and did not know her till she had brought forth her firstborn Son. And he called His name Jesus.

St. Luke tells in Chapter 2 of his Gospel:

And it came to pass in those days, that a decree went out from Caesar Augustus that all the world should be registered. This census first took place while Quirinius was governing Syria. So all went to be registered, everyone to his own city. And Joseph also went up from Gallilee, out of the city of Nazareth, into Judea, to the city of David, which is called Bethlehem, because he was of the house and lineage of David, to be registered with Mary, his betrothed wife, who was with child. So it was, that while they were there, the days were completed for her to be delivered. And she brought forth her firstborn Son, and wrapped him in swaddling cloths, and laid him in a manger, because there was no room for them in the inn. Now there were in the same country shepherds living out in the field, keeping watch over their flock by night. And behold, an angel of the Lord stood before them, and the glory of the Lord shone around them, and they were greatly afraid. Then the angel said to them, 'Do not be afraid, for behold, I bring you good tidings of great joy which shall be to all people. For there is born to you this day in the city of David a Savior, who is Christ the Lord. And this will be the sign for you: You will find a Babe wrapped in swaddling cloths, lying in a manger.' And suddenly there was with the angel a multitude of the heavenly host praising God and saying, 'Glory to God in the highest, and on earth peace, good will toward men.

There it is, right from God's Word, what Christmas really means. Christmas is a time to reflect on God's great Gift to the world which he loved so much that he unveiled His plan for man's salvation through the birth of Jesus. This Christmas, read the whole story as told in Matthew 2 and Luke 2. Ponder God's love for mankind—and for you—let it fill your heart and mind; then pass that love along to others. The writer of these "Potluck" articles wishes everyone a most joyous holiday season!

126

PROPHETIC WORDS

ABOUT THE FUTURE
(May 8, 1986)

(Author's Note: Today's article is an unusual one, pertaining to a world-wide historical event with religious importance, linked to Biblical references, and providing food for thought for the times in which we live. The article was prepared from data and with photos provided by my son, Nathan Krupp, and his wife Joanne, who were among twelve people from the United States participating in the event in Israel.)

One-hundred fifty-three prophets, prophetesses, and intercessors, representing every continent, and from many different denominational backgrounds, met on Mount Carmel, Israel, March 17–22, 1986, to seek the Lord. "It was a time of deep humbling, repentance, and prayer as we sought to be pure before God, and come into unity with each other," Nate reported. To refresh readers' memories, Mt. Carmel is in the northern part of Israel.

He went on to say that the message that came forth as they waited upon the Lord was that the "great shaking" mentioned in Hebrews 12:25-29 had begun. This passage states: "For if those did not escape when they refused him who warned them on earth, much less shall we escape who turn away from Him who warns from heaven. And His voice shook the earth then, but now He has promised, saying, 'Yet once more I will shake not only the earth, but also the heaven.' And this expression, 'Yet once more,' denotes the removing of those things which can be shaken, as of created things, in order that those things which cannot be shaken may remain. Therefore, since we receive a Kingdom which cannot be shaken, let us show gratitude, by which we may offer to God an acceptable service with reverence and awe; for our God is a consuming fire."

The initial Mt. Carmel gathering was followed by a second gathering in Jerusalem, March 23–30, of 1,500 people from forty nations. During that week, the word and inspiration that was received on Mt. Carmel was shared with the larger group to take back to their various countries. Nate spoke at that conference and said, "God is going to shake the earth. All of the works of man will crumble. The only thing that will remain is Christ's Kingdom."

To refresh readers' memories it is suggested that they read 1 Kings, Chapter 18. It was there that Elijah the prophet, on Mt. Carmel, demonstrated to the followers of Baal the greatness and power of God. The followers of Baal called upon their god to send down fire to burn the bullock offering they had prepared, but without success. Elijah called upon God to consume the offering he had prepared. The Bible says, "Then the fire of the Lord fell, and consumed the burnt sacrifice, and the wood and the stones, and the dust, and licked up the water that was in the trench. And when all the people saw it, they fell on their faces; and they said, 'the Lord, he is the God; the Lord he is the God.'"

Today, it is believed that the top of Mt. Carmel, where there is a statue of Elijah, is not the spot where the miracle was performed. Rather, that it occurred further down the mountain. Someone believed there had to be a well fed by a spring near the site and did discover it along with a natural amphitheater where the 850 prophets of Baal could have easily gathered, at a lower elevation, not the top.

Joanne, Nate's wife, heard further information to further confirm the authenticity of the lower elevation. The story goes that a visitor to Mt. Carmel was looking the lower site over, and as he was walking along, kicked over a stone which was a shiny green color. Picking it up, he tried to scratch it with his wife's diamond, but to no avail. The man took it to geologist friend in Tel Aviv and inquired if he could tell him what is was. The geologist didn't know, but told the man that the stone was not native to Israel. The geologist asked that the rock be left with him for a week for analysis. The finder of the stone agreed,

Prophets and intercessors in 1986 at the site on Mt. Carmel where the prophets of Baal were unable to match God's miracle of sending down fire to consume an offering. (See 1 Kings, Chapter 18.)

but told him, "I did find it in Israel, but I'll not tell you where until you have analyzed it." Returning a week later, the geologist reported the stone worthless, but said, "The one thing I can tell you is that this rock has undergone a tremendous heat, like a nuclear explosion, and the green color has been caused by something like a nuclear fusion." Then, the man revealed to the geologist where he had found the rock—where God's fire had fallen!

The intent of today's article, other than to inform readers of the importance of the coming together of people from many nations to pray together to God for guidance, and to consider common interests, should be obvious. Here are three of my views briefed:

1. God's time-table tells us that we are living in the so-called "last days," prior to the great-shaking by God, and the return of Christ to establish His Kingdom on earth.

2. God's word has revealed his wishes for man, and there is still time for repentance, and preparation for the "last days."

3. For America and its population, the future view is awesome unless there are changes in lifestyles.

In short, we must return to God—and to His Book, the Bible.

Visit us at
arcadiapublishing.com

www.ingramcontent.com/pod-product-compliance
Lightning Source LLC
Chambersburg PA
CBHW050622110426
42813CB00007B/1692

* 9 7 8 1 5 3 1 6 1 3 5 9 4 *